Freedom Just Around the Corner

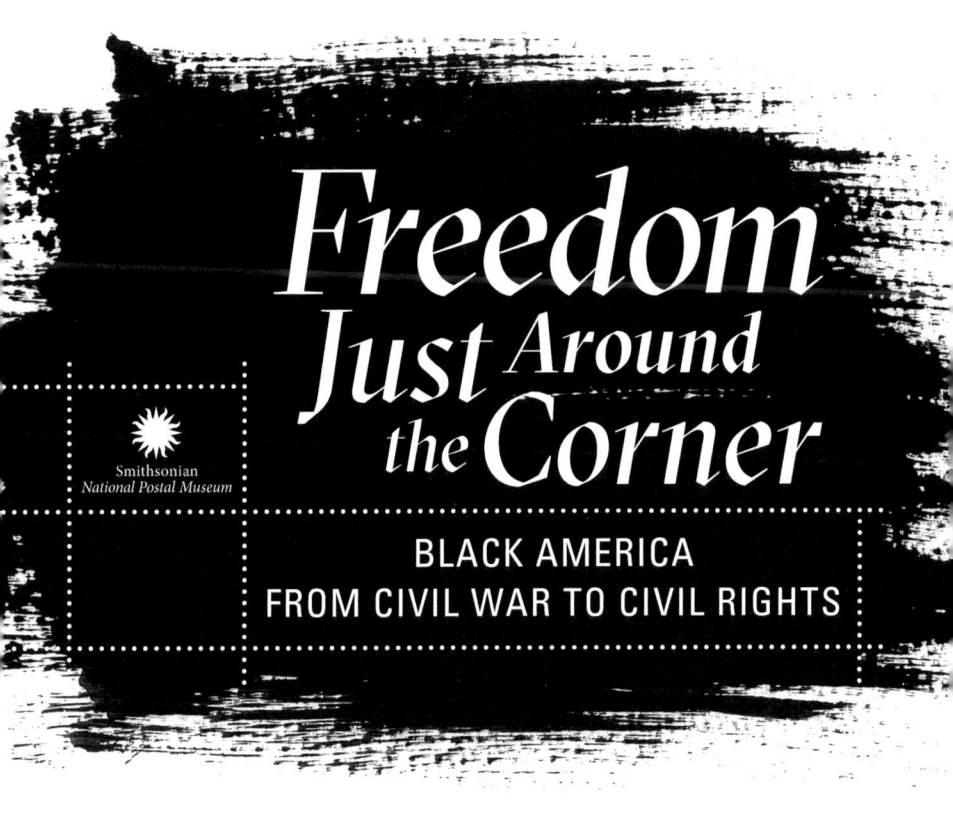

DANIEL PIAZZA

FEBRUARY 12, 2015–FEBRUARY 15, 2016

SMITHSONIAN NATIONAL POSTAL MUSEUM
WASHINGTON, D.C.

Smithsonian National Postal Museum
2 Massachusetts Avenue, N.E.
MRC 570 PO Box 37012
Washington, D.C. 20013-7012

www.postalmuseum.si.edu

Published in conjunction with the exhibition
*Freedom Just Around the Corner: Black America
from Civil War to Civil Rights* organized by the
Smithsonian National Postal Museum
February 12, 2015–February 15, 2016

Copyright © 2014 by Smithsonian National Postal Museum

ISBN: 978-0-692-36592-2

Design by Christine Lefebvre Design

Printed by Minuteman Press, Toledo, Ohio

Contents

FOREWORD	8
SLAVE-CARRIED MAIL	10
ABOLITION AND THE MAIL	20
CIVIL WAR	34
RECONSTRUCTION	44
SEGREGATION	54
CIVIL RIGHTS MOVEMENT	70
BLACK HERITAGE STAMP SERIES	86
CURATOR'S AFTERWORD	100
SPONSOR MESSAGE	101
ACKNOWLEDGEMENTS	102

Company E, 4th U.S. Colored Infantry at Washington, D.C.'s Fort Lincoln c. 1862–1865

COURTESY LIBRARY OF CONGRESS PRINTS AND PHOTOGRAPHS DIVISION

You cannot make soldiers of slaves, or slaves of soldiers. The day you make a soldier of them is the beginning of the end...then our whole theory of slavery is wrong.

CONFEDERATE MAJOR GENERAL
HOWELL COBB, 1865

Foreword

It is hard for me to believe that nearly a year and a half has passed since we opened the William H. Gross Stamp Gallery.

The results of the Gross Stamp Gallery have been unbelievable. Our attendance was up forty percent. Eighty-five percent of our visitors said they would return for another visit. Most importantly, more than one-quarter of our visitors leave here inspired to take up stamp collecting as a hobby.

The gallery continues to generate tremendous coverage. It has been featured in the *New York Times*, *Wall Street Journal*, and *Washington Post*. Television crews from C-SPAN, CBS Sunday Morning, and Fox 5 DC have broadcast from here. Each new exhibit we open, including our forthcoming display of the famed British Guiana Penny Magenta, is another opportunity to promote philately.

Before I came to the Smithsonian Institution I had a career with the U.S. Postal Service that lasted nearly forty years. USPS is proud of its history as one of the country's largest employers of African Americans. That story is told in *Freedom Just Around the Corner* and the exhibits on the museum's lower level. I hope that you will enjoy them.

ALLEN R. KANE
DIRECTOR

The National Postal Museum's first exhibition devoted entirely to African American history, *Freedom* marks 150 years since the end of the Civil War and the abolition of slavery throughout the United States.

It highlights letters carried by enslaved Americans, mail sent by and to leaders of the civil rights movement, and original artwork for numerous stamps issued by the United States Postal Service. Nearly one hundred items from National Postal Museum's collection are on display, augmented by outstanding pieces on loan from other institutions and private collections.

News was usually gotten from the colored man who was sent to the post-office for the mail. In our case the post-office was about three miles from the plantation and the mail came once or twice a week.

BOOKER T. WASHINGTON,
UP FROM SLAVERY, 1901

Slave-Carried Mail

Before the introduction of home mail delivery, slaves often carried letters to and from the post office. Slave-carried mail is usually identified by a notation—called an *endorsement*—that also served as a travel pass. These mail messengers could be an important source of news if they overheard discussions during their travels.

1619-1865

▾ "Sent girl Susan" stampless folded letter APRIL 16, 1850

Susan was probably unaware that the letter she carried to the Eastville, Virginia post office contained arrangements for her to be sold to a slave dealer in Richmond.

> *I send to you my negro girl Susan aged 16 all rite and a first rate girl big limbs and muscles please sell her and remit...*

▸ Littleton Dennis Teackle stampless cover c. 1822–1836
LOAN FROM SCOTT R. TREPEL

A slave named Moses carried this letter and a trunk to Annapolis, Maryland where Teackle was a member of the state legislature.

Freedom Just Around the Corner

▲ **"Servant girl Lucile" stamped envelope** c. 1853–1860
LOAN FROM SCOTT R. TREPEL

The addressee, Rice Carter Ballard, was a slave dealer who owned plantations in Louisiana, Arkansas, and Mississippi.

▼ Mrs. Maria Gooch stampless cover
DECEMBER 22, 1856   LOAN FROM SCOTT R. TREPEL

A cart and three slaves—Turner, Lindsay, and Julia—brought this letter with them to Airfield Plantation near Richmond, Virginia. It was not uncommon for slaves to be given travel passes at Christmastime to visit friends and relatives on other plantations.

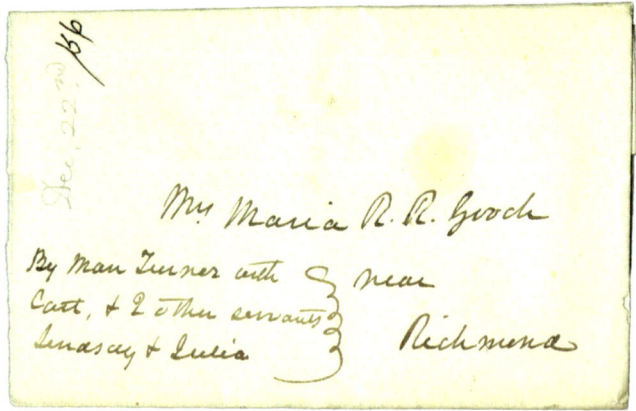

▼ "Davy Lamar (colored)" stampless letter
UNDATED   LOAN FROM DAVID MIELKE

Slaves occasionally received mail, as evidenced by the endorsement on this letter: "Mr. Wells will please read the enclosed note to Davy."

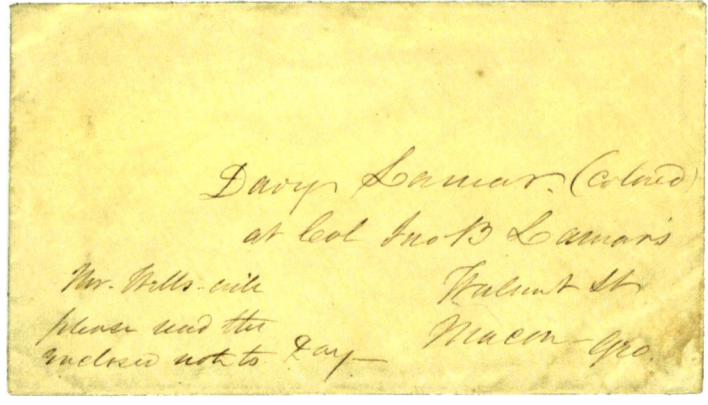

Freedom Just Around the Corner

The Business of Slavery

American slavery was big business. On the eve of the Civil War, four million slaves produced cash crops—cotton, tobacco, and rice—that were exported at high prices. In addition to the crops they raised, slaves themselves were commodities to be bought, sold, bred, and borrowed against. A variety of service industries supported the slave economy including dealers, insurance companies, and shippers. The federal government also derived revenue from taxes on the sale of slaves and the export of slave-grown products.

Slave dealer's shop on Whitehall (now Peachtree) Street, Atlanta 1864
COURTESY LIBRARY OF CONGRESS PRINTS AND PHOTOGRAPHS DIVISION

Davis, Deupree and Company cover and letter OCTOBER 13, 1860

Richmond, Virginia was the center of the domestic slave trade on the eve of the Civil War. Despite the large volume of mail that must have been sent by slave dealers, just a few examples survive today.

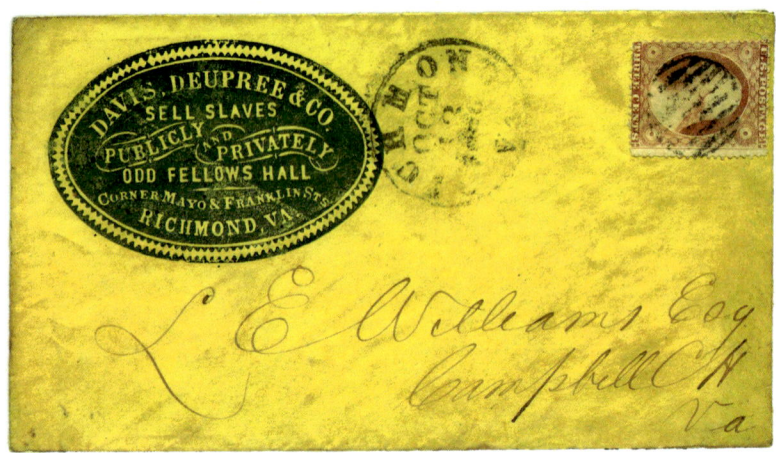

Freedom Just Around the Corner

> Richmond Octo 12 1860
>
> Dear Sir
>
> Our market is fair at this time several here who wish to buy some good negroes, say good girls, and we have been keeping them waiting for you, Expecting you in as soon as you got our letter, But as you have not arrived we Concluded you did not get our letter. Come in immediately —
>
> Very resp'y
> Davis, Dupree & Co

Our market is fair at this time several here who wish to buy some good negroes...

This Indenture made this the 3º day of March 1863, between Margaret Jones of the first part and David Clark of the second part & both of the County of Henderson and State of Kentucky witnesseth that whereas the said Clark has loaned to L. F. Jones the sum of six hundred dollars, as evidenced by a promisory note of this date payable with interest at six months from date, signed by the said L. F. Jones and Margaret Jones of the first part, the said sum of money to be paid to said Jones on the delivery of this deed, and whereas the party of the first part in consideration of said loan and as an inducement thereto has agreed to give the further security herein set forth — Now in consideration of the premises, the party of the first part, has sold and hereby conveys in mortgage to the party of the second part, her negro man, named George, of Copper color and aged about forty five years — The condition of this conveyance is that if the said L. F. Jones and Margaret Jones shall well and truly pay off and discharge said debt, it shall be void — else to remain in full force and virtue —

In Testimony whereof the party of the first part has hereunto set her hand and affixed her seal, the day and year above written.

Margaret X Jones
her mark

◀ **First Federal Issue revenue stamps on slave mortgage document** MARCH 3, 1863
LOAN FROM HERMANN IVESTER

Kentucky slaveowner Margaret Jones secured a loan of $600 by mortgaging her "negro man, named George, of copper color and aged about forty five years." Under the terms, George would be deeded back to Jones if the loan was paid off in six months.

▼ **First Federal Issue revenue stamps on slave sale document** OCTOBER 1, 1863
LOAN FROM MICHAEL MAHLER

A total of six cents tax was due on $305 paid for a "negro boy Charles" at a court-ordered auction in Bourbon County, Kentucky.

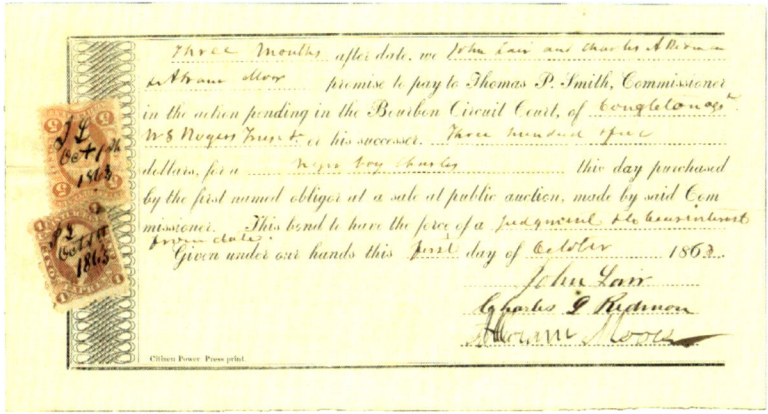

BLACK AMERICA FROM CIVIL WAR TO CIVIL RIGHTS

The New Method of Sorting the Mail, As Practiced by Southern Slave-Holders 1835

The Charleston, South Carolina post office was raided by a pro-slavery mob in July 1835. "U.S.M." on the mail bag at lower left stands for U.S. Mail, and the mob is burning bundles of abolitionist newspapers—with the help of the city postmaster.

Abolition and the Mail

The political ideals of the American Revolution—liberty, equality, and freedom—inspired some Americans to rethink the morality of slavery. By 1804, reformers had succeeded in abolishing slavery in the northern states and turned all their efforts to attacking slavery in the south and opposing its spread in the west. Postage rates decreased from the 1830s through the 1850s, allowing abolitionists to distribute literature cheaply via the post office. Many southerners regarded these mail campaigns as an attack, aided and abetted by the federal government.

"Great Meeting in Fanueil Hall" circular
FEBRUARY 5, 1842 LOAN FROM JOHN M. HOTCHNER

Boston abolitionists met in 1842 and called on Congress to end slavery in Washington, D.C. This report of the meeting was mailed free to a member of Congress with an affixed seal that reads: "Are you a FREEMAN... *Do* as you would be *done by*. Proclaim liberty to the captives." Slavery remained legal in the District until 1862.

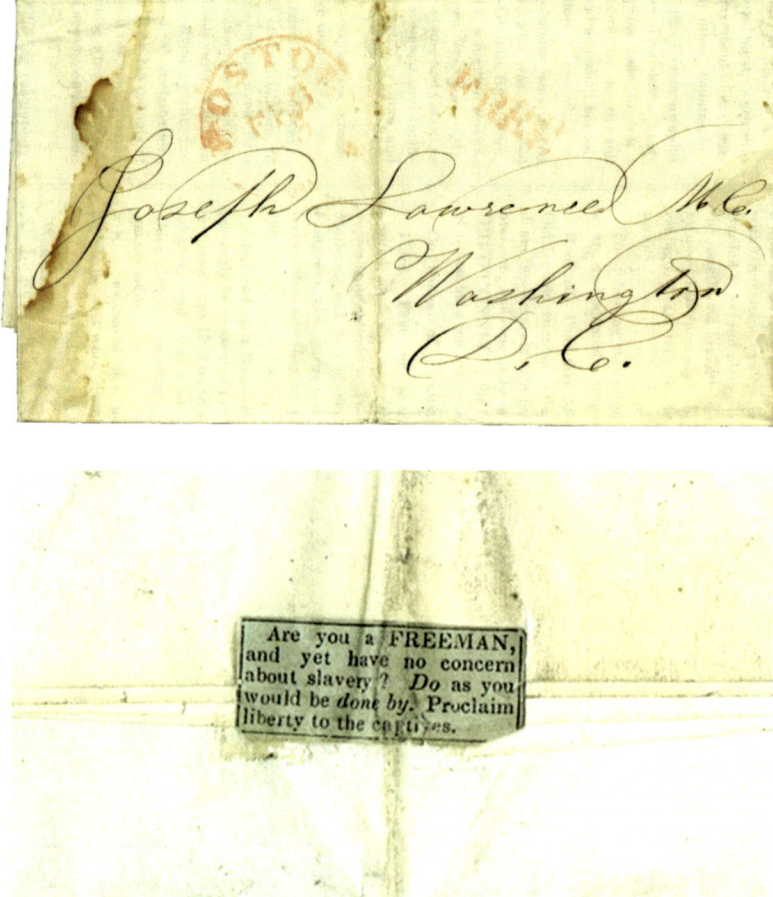

Great Meeting in Faneuil Hall, for the abolition of Slavery in the District of Columbia.

A large and overwhelming Meeting of the citizens of Boston and vicinity was held in the old Cradle of Liberty, on Friday evening, Jan. 28, 1842, favorable to the immediate abolition of Slavery in the District of Columbia, and, on motion of Edmund Quincy, The Meeting was called to order by FRANCIS JACKSON, and WILLIAM LLOYD GARRISON was unanimously called to the Chair.

On motion, *Voted*, That there be chosen six Vice Presidents, to be nominated by the Chair. The following persons were then chosen, viz :

FRANCIS JACKSON,
JOSEPH SOUTHWICK, } Of Massachusetts.
GEORGE BRADBURN,
COL. J. P. MILLER, of Vermont.
NATHANIEL P. ROGERS, of New Hampshire.
JAMES CANNINGS FULLER, of New York.

The following persons were then appointed Secretaries, viz:

WILLIAM BASSETT, of Lynn,
CHARLES LENOX REMOND, of Salem,
HENRY W. WILLIAMS, of Boston.

The Chairman said he would beg leave to present to the Meeting, for their consideration, the following Resolutions, which expressed the feelings of his own bosom, and the spirit of which he thought should animate the bosom of every friend of Liberty :

1. *Resolved*, That inasmuch as the District of Columbia is neither a part nor under the control of any one State, but belongs to the people of the United States, and is under the exclusive jurisdiction of Congress in all cases whatsoever, it follows that, for the existence of slavery in that District, Congress and the people of the United States are directly responsible ; and at any moment they can constitutionally abolish it.

2. *Resolved*, That, in the awful name of the God of nations, and by every consideration of justice, humanity and religion, we call upon Congress immediately to break the fetters and to undo the heavy burdens which that body has made, and to let the oppressed go free, in the aforesaid District ; and to give no countenance or protection to slavery in any part of the republic.

3. *Resolved*, That the refusal of Congress to receive the petitions of the people, in relation to this great national iniquity and curse, is an act of high-handed usurpation, flagrantly unconstitutional, and not to be endured by a free people ; and, if persisted in much longer, must necessarily lead to the most deplorable consequences.

4. *Resolved*, That the insolent rejection, by Congress, of the resolutions of the Legislatures of Vermont and Massachusetts, in relation to slavery in the District of Columbia, is a bold denial of the sovereignty of those States, a most alarming precedent in the legislation of the country, and a plain demonstration of the fact, that northern liberty is but the football of the slaveholding power.

5. *Resolved*, That the Legislatures of Vermont and Massachusetts cannot tamely submit to such indignities without great criminality, and the exhibition of a cowardly and truckling spirit; and that, by their allegiance to the principles of the Constitution, by a due regard to their own character, and by the respect which they entertain for their own constituents, they are bound to enter a solemn protest against this despotic procedure, and to warn Congress to pause before again perpetrating it in the manner aforesaid.

6. *Resolved*, That the thanks of the friends of liberty, universally, and especially in Massachusetts, are due to John Quincy Adams, for his bold, faithful and indefatigable advocacy of the right of petition, under circumstances of great difficulty and peril; and that the Secretaries of this meeting be requested to forward a copy of this resolution to MR. ADAMS, in the name of this meeting, as a slight token of its high appreciation of his conduct in such an emergency, and of its determination to sustain him in every constitutional effort that he may make in favor of the rights of man, irrespective of complexional differences.

7. *Resolved*, That when the Senators and Representatives of this Commonwealth, in Congress, find themselves deprived of the liberty of speech on its floor, and prohibited from defending the right of their constituents to petition that body in a constitutional manner, they ought at once to withdraw, and return to their several homes, leaving the people of Massachusetts to devise such ways and means for a redress of their grievances as they shall deem necessary.

8. *Resolved*, That the union of Liberty and Slavery, in one just and equal compact, is that which it is not in the power of God or men to achieve, because it is a moral impossibility, as much as the peaceful amalgamation of fire and gunpowder ; and, therefore, the American Union is such only in form, but not in substance—a hollow mockery instead of a glorious reality.

9. *Resolved*, That if the South be madly bent upon perpetuating her atrocious slave system, and thereby

5¢ Franklin on Free Soil Party circular
SEPTEMBER 1848

The Free Soil Party was a third party in the presidential election of 1848, when Martin Van Buren was their candidate. Their sole platform was preventing the spread of slavery into the new territories acquired during the Mexican-American War. The first U.S. postage stamp, issued in 1847, was used to send their political circular through the mail.

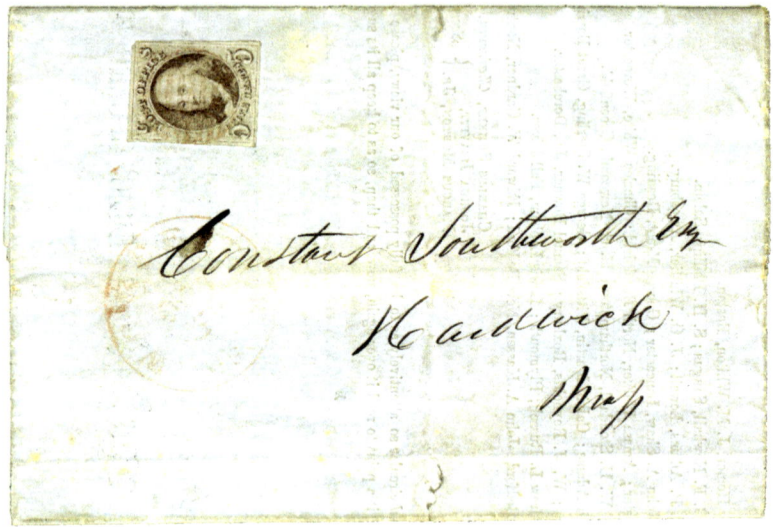

[CONFIDENTIAL CIRCULAR.]

BOSTON, SEPTEMBER 15, 1848.
6 Massachusetts Block, Court Square.

DEAR SIR,

WILL you do so much for the cause of Free Soil as to aid the State Committee to the extent of deliberately reading this letter through, which will occupy not exceeding ten minutes of your valuable time.

The Free Soil party of Massachusetts is now fairly entered upon the campaign. We have an approved State Ticket — PHILLIPS & MILLS — men surpassed by no others in their zeal for the good cause, and their qualifications for public service. We have also an Electoral Ticket of true men, pledged to the support of

VAN BUREN AND ADAMS.

Never was a party formed upon a better basis than the *Buffalo Platform*. Never was a party furnished with candidates more deserving of public confidence, or more true to the platform which they represent. It remains that we do our duty, our whole duty, to secure their election.

If we would act efficiently, we must be *organized*. It is impossible to bring out our whole strength without systematic and combined efforts, on a regular and judicious *plan*. The following plan is earnestly recommended to be adopted in every town.

The State Committee believe that the uniform adoption of this plan, in every town, if faithfully carried out, will secure the State vote for Free soil, at the coming election. We hope no town will voluntarily or carelessly incur the responsibility of endangering defeat by inaction.

PLAN OF ORGANIZATION.

1. A *County Committee*, consisting of a few men, centrally and conveniently situated, so that they can consult and act together, and can easily reach every town, by letter, or personal visits.

2. In addition, the Chairman of each *Town Committee* may be *ex officio* a member of the County Committee.

3. The County Committee, by its *Chairman or Secretary*, *will be in correspondence with the State Committee*, communicating at once the names of its officers, to be entered on the State Committee's books, and furnishing needful information, at all times.

4. The County Committee will furnish to the State Committee the *names of the Chairmen of Town Committees*, and also the name of a trusty person, residing in the neighborhood of each Post Office, to whom circulars, extras, &c. may be sent, when necessary.

5. This *trusty correspondent* should either be a person who is in the constant practice of getting promptly his letters coming by every mail, or he should make it a point to do so, at any rate, during the campaign, so that information sent may not be useless in the Post Office.

6. The *County Committee* should see to the proper call of county conventions, and also take measures, when needful, for mass meetings in the county. They should encourage the county press, and see to the furnishing of publications, gratuitously, or by sale. They should see that every town is organized, and ought to have every town visited, at least once a year, by members, in person, or by an agent, who will see the most active men, and encourage and aid them to go forward.

7. The *Town Committee* will take the lead in the political action of the town; such as the choice of delegates to State, County, or District Conventions, and the nomination of representatives. They will also, if necessary, get up lectures, neighborhood meetings, lyceum discussions, circulate papers and tracts, &c.

Less than a year after its publication in the United States, *Uncle Tom's Cabin* sold more than one million copies in Great Britain. Although modern critics point out the book's use of racially stereotyped characters, in its day it was regarded as a powerful piece of anti-slavery propaganda. Scenes from the novel decorate the reverse of this British anti-slavery cover published by James Valentine of Dundee, Scotland.

▸ ***Uncle Tom's Cabin* illustrated anti-slavery cover** MARCH 28, 1853

▾ **Early London edition of *Uncle Tom's Cabin*** 1852

LOAN FROM SMITHSONIAN INSTITUTION LIBRARIES, DIBNER LIBRARY OF THE HISTORY OF SCIENCE AND TECHNOLOGY

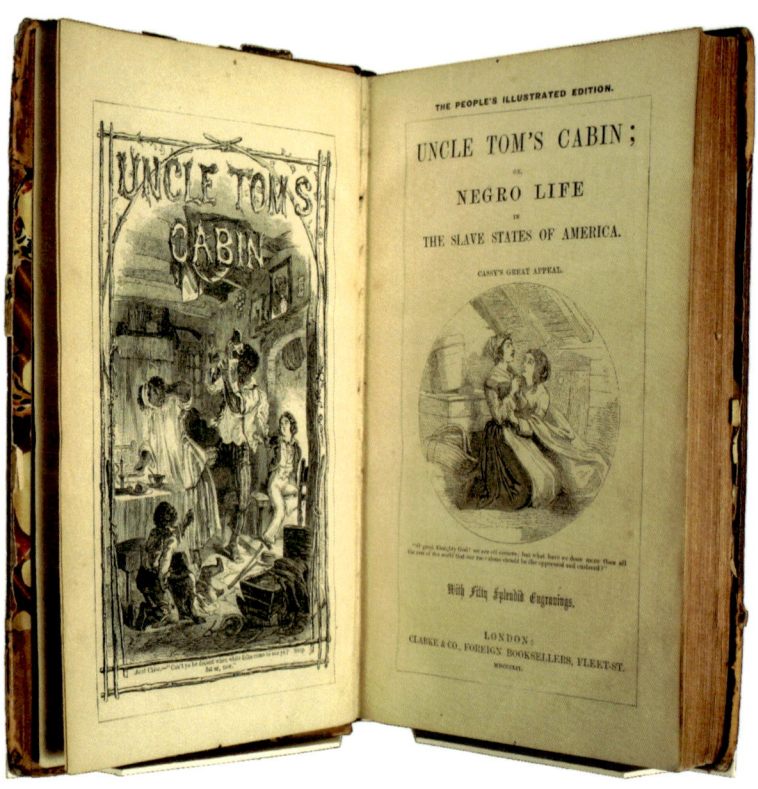

26   *Freedom Just Around the Corner*

The scenes, clockwise from top flap: Uncle Tom is sold away from Aunt Chloe and his children because of his owner's bankruptcy. The overseers Sambo and Quimbo flog Uncle Tom. Simon Legree whips Uncle Tom. Uncle Tom reads his Bible atop cotton bales on a Mississippi River steamboat. Pursued by slave catchers, Eliza escapes north with her five year old son Harry. Emmeline is sold away from her grieving mother, Susan.

The U.S. and Great Britain prohibited the importation of slaves in 1807. Both nations established Africa *Squadrons*—naval detachments to intercept slave trading ships off the West African coast. Slaves found on the captured vessels were freed, usually in Liberia. Mail to and from ships of the Africa Squadron is quite scarce.

▼ Cover from USS *Portsmouth* off Cape Verde   JANUARY 7, 1849
LOAN FROM PATRICK MASELIS

◄ USS *Portsmouth*
COURTESY LIBRARY OF CONGRESS PRINTS AND PHOTOGRAPHS DIVISION

Freedom Just Around the Corner

▾ Cover to USS *Mohican* off Angola DECEMBER 20, 1860
LOAN FROM PATRICK MASELIS

Mohican's only capture was the slave ship *Erie*, carrying almost 900 Africans. The thirty-three cents postage on this letter paid five cents domestic U.S. postage, the sixteen cents transatlantic ship rate, and twelve cents (equal to six pence) British Empire postage.

Liberia

While abolitionists wanted an immediate and unconditional end to slavery, the American Colonization Society (ACS) supported gradual emancipation combined with resettling freed slaves in Africa. This appealed to slave owners who feared rebellions; white farmers and laborers who worried that free black labor would depress wages; religious leaders who wanted to missionize Africa; and those who believed freed slaves would never be treated fairly in America. The ACS founded the West African colony of Liberia in 1822 and resettled more than 13,000 freed American slaves there.

3¢ Landing of the First Colonists, Liberia 1949

Signed by their designer, the noted illustrator Arthur Szyk, these stamps romanticize the arrival of the first African Americans at Liberia in 1821. Most of the 164 emigrants on board the ship *Nautilus* (visible in the background) were from North Carolina and were under eighteen years old. Within a year, 25% died from malaria.

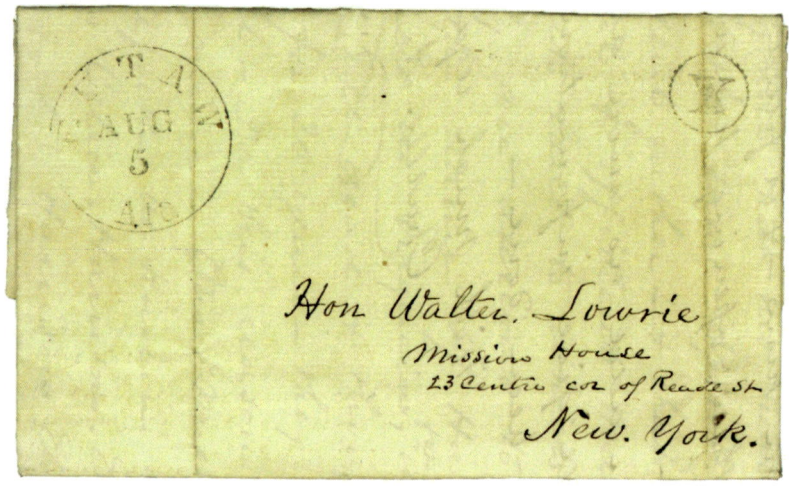

◆ **Presbyterian Board of Foreign Missions stampless folded letter** AUGUST 5, 1846

Reverend Charles A. Stillman, a minister in Alabama, reports in his letter that local colonizationists have purchased a slave family's freedom for $2500 in order to send them to Liberia as missionaries.

They are all fond of the name of Harrison—that of their first owners in Virginia, for whom... they cherish a tender regard. For this reason they desire to retain that name. Our missionary therefore will henceforth be known as Ellis Harrison...

Liberian stampless folded letter c. 1852

The writer, James M. Priest, was born a slave in Kentucky. Freed by his owner to become a missionary in Liberia, he later served as the fledgling country's vice president and a justice of its supreme court. His letter entered the U.S. aboard a ship that landed at Baltimore.

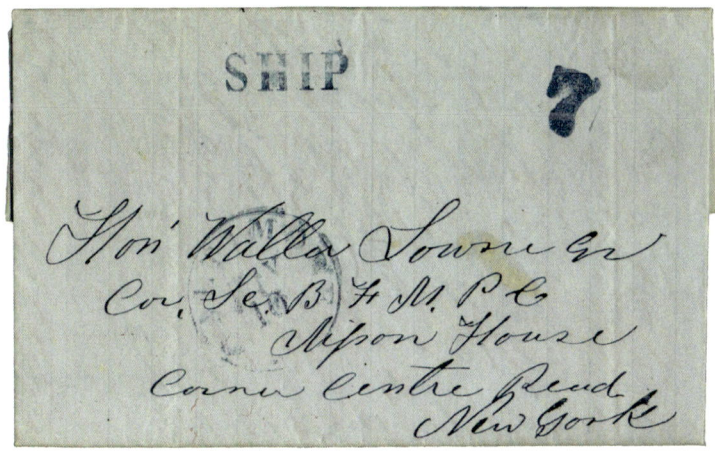

James M. Priest daguerreotype portrait by Augustus Washington
c. 1856–1860
COURTESY LIBRARY OF CONGRESS PRINTS AND PHOTOGRAPHS DIVISION

BLACK AMERICA FROM CIVIL WAR TO CIVIL RIGHTS

Soldiers in winter camp c. 1864
COURTESY LIBRARY OF CONGRESS PRINTS AND PHOTOGRAPHS DIVISION

Civil War

1861-1865

The debate over slavery turned violent during the 1850s. Pro- and anti-slavery settlers in the Kansas Territory fought a year-long running battle known as "Bleeding Kansas." An abortive attempt at a slave rebellion in Virginia, followed closely by Abraham Lincoln's election as president in 1860, made the Civil War inevitable. Although roughly 10% of Union forces were African American, they served in segregated units led by white officers.

▼ Captain John Brown cover NOVEMBER 29, 1859

John Brown was a veteran of Bleeding Kansas who organized an 1859 attack on the federal armory at Harpers Ferry in hopes of inciting a Virginia slave rebellion. His capture, trial, and execution became a cause célèbre that brought pro- and anti-slavery arguments to a fever pitch. During his final month in jail at Charlestown, Virginia, Brown was allowed to send and receive mail.

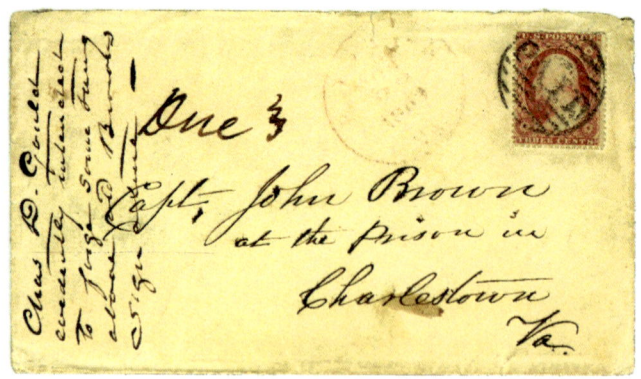

▼ "Beardless" Lincoln campaign cover c. 1861

Slavery Sectional, Freedom National—an abolitionist slogan coined by U.S. Senator Charles Sumner of Massachusetts—here endorses Abraham Lincoln's 1860 presidential candidacy. The sentiment proved prophetic; Lincoln's election without the support of a single southern state led to the secession of the Confederate States of America and the Civil War.

Early in the Civil War, Union General Benjamin Butler decreed that escaped slaves who reached his station at Fort Monroe would be considered "contraband" and not returned to their owners. Although the idea of black troops is caricatured by these envelopes, nearly 200,000 black men served in the Union forces.

▼ "Come back here you black rascal" illustrated cover c. 1861 LOAN FROM SCOTT R. TREPEL

▼ Runaway slaves volunteering for Union army illustrated cover c. 1861

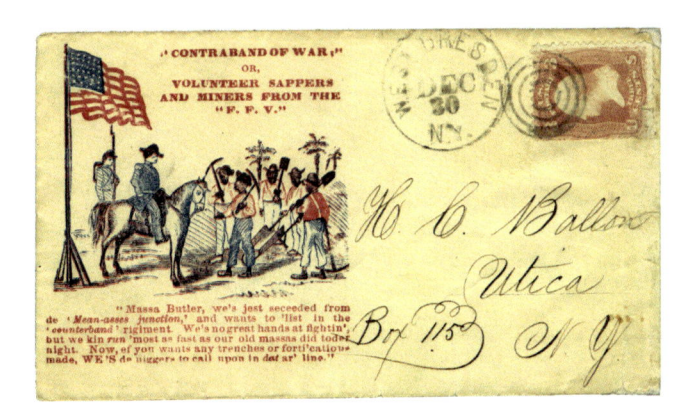

BLACK AMERICA FROM CIVIL WAR TO CIVIL RIGHTS

▶ First Federal Issue revenue stamps on deed of emancipation MAY 9, 1864
LOAN FROM HOWARD COUNTY HISTORICAL SOCIETY

Seventeen-year-old Maryland slave William H. Jones enlisted in the 19th Regiment, U.S. Colored Troops on December 18, 1863. His owner later filed emancipation papers, possibly to apply for federal compensation. Wounded during the siege of Petersburg, Virginia, Jones was discharged and returned to Maryland.

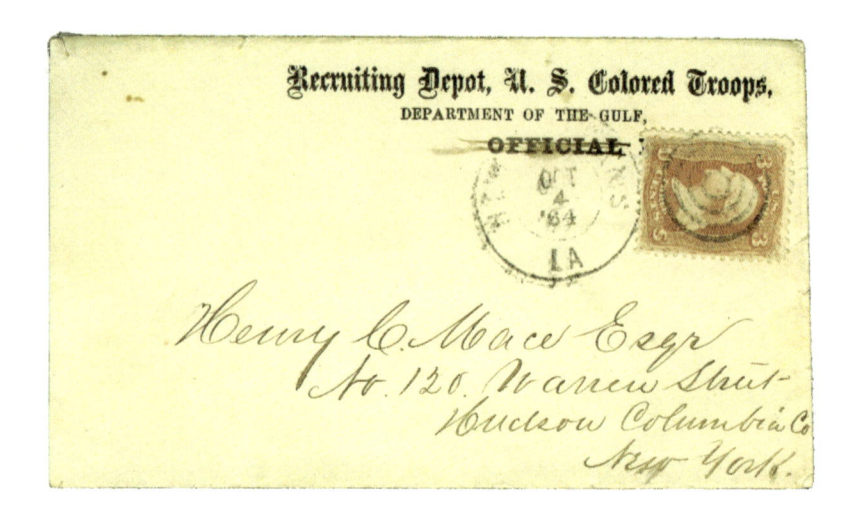

▲ U.S. Colored Troops Recruiting Depot cover OCTOBER 4, 1864

Recruiting depots paid new recruits an enlistment bounty, mustered them into Union service, and assigned them to a regiment. Most black troops served as manual laborers or on guard duty, including guarding Confederate prisoners of war. The Department of the Gulf was headquartered in occupied New Orleans.

E.

DEED OF MANUMISSION AND RELEASE OF SERVICE.

Whereas my slave _Wm H Jones_ has enlisted in the service of the United States: now, in consideration thereof, I, _Wm Hughes_, of _Howard_ County, State of _Maryland_, do hereby, in consideration of said enlistment, manumit, set free, and release the above-named _Wm H Jones_ from all service due me; his freedom to commence from the _Thirty first of December 1863_, the date of his enlistment as aforesaid in the _Nineteenth_ Regiment of Colored Troops, in the service of the United States.

Witness my hand and seal, this _Ninth_ day of _May_, 1864.

Wm Hughes [SEAL]

Witness:
S. Sykes
Charles W. White

Howard County,
State of Maryland, 1864.
Before me appeared this day _William Hughes_ and acknowledged the above Deed of Manumission and Release of Service to be his free act and deed.

S. Sykes J.P.

121st U.S. Colored Infantry Regiment cover and letter

DECEMBER 21, 1864
LOAN FROM JOHN M. HOTCHNER

The 121st consisted almost entirely of black troops raised in Kentucky, where one of the regiment's white officers mailed this letter shortly before a skirmish with Confederate soldiers.

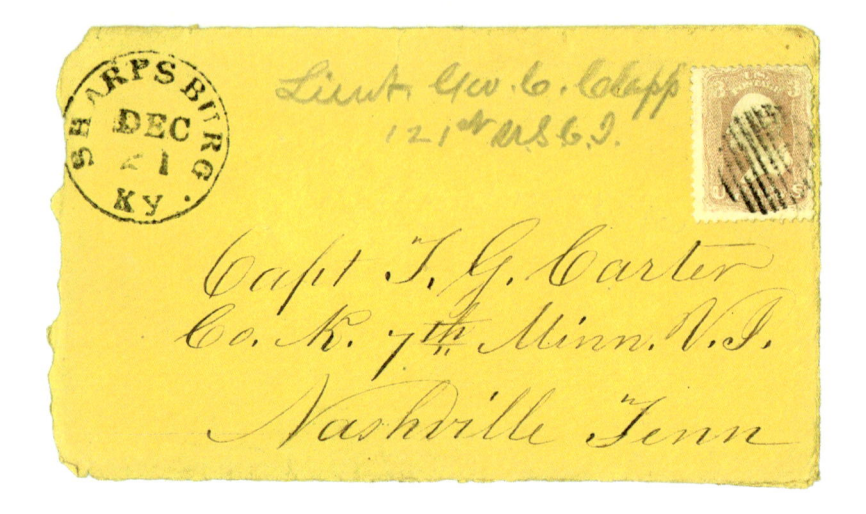

> *Nothing suits me better than to have command of Darkey Troops... It is a fact that colored Troops learn faster than white Troops.*

Hd. Qrs. Recruiting Detachment
121st U.S.C.I. Sharpsburg Dec 22. 1864

Capt T. G. Carter,
Co. K. 7th Minn. V.I.

Dear Captain

Your kind favor of Dec 8th reached me fifth days ago and through the hurry of business on hand at the time could not answer it till now.

I thank you for the interest you have taken in my welfare and that of my family by sending Check on New York for 103.74/100 dollars – it came in good time to relieve all my present wants, and really is a great favor on your part – Be assured I appreciate such favors.

I was very glad to hear from you – to know that you were well and where you were, as the 7th has been constantly on the move since ordered south from Paducah Ky. You know very well how much attached I had become by 2 years service to the 7th Regiment and perhaps can appreciate in some degree my feelings on being compelled to leave you on the Levee at Memphis Tenn. for a birth in Convalescent Camp Ft Pickering. It is true that I suffered while there, and after getting a furlough of 30 days the 18th of July I suffered while at home two months passing through intermittant remitt ant and typhoid fever. I was during the time useless as a soldier, or for anything else, and when the order arrived, ordering me detached from my Regiment and to proceed without delay to Bainbridge Hd. Qrs. I was hardly able to comply, and had an extension of furlough 20 days.

▸ **William H. Carney Medal of Honor** 1900 LOAN FROM CARL J. CRUZ

William Harvey Carney, born a slave in Virginia in 1840, volunteered for the celebrated, all-black 54th Massachusetts Volunteer Infantry Regiment. Shot twice while rescuing the American flag during an attack on Battery Wagner near Charleston, South Carolina, he later received the Medal of Honor. After the war, he worked as a letter carrier in the New Bedford, Massachusetts post office for more than thirty years.

▴ **William H. Carney on his postal route** c. 1880
COURTESY CARL J. CRUZ

42   *Freedom Just Around the Corner*

▾ Confederate "turned" cover c. 1862

As the Civil War dragged on, southerners "turned" unused documents and even leftover wallpaper inside out to fashion homemade envelopes. This cover, mailed in Georgia with Confederate postage, was made from a tax assessment form that lists "Slaves–Male" as property to be taxed.

▾ Confederate "Office Enrollment of Slaves" cover c. 1864 LOAN FROM SCOTT R. TREPEL

Robert E. Lee ordered conscription of slaves in 1864 to bolster his faltering Confederate army. General Howell Cobb, well-known for his opposition to enlisting slaves, was placed in charge of doing just that in Georgia. This letter to Cobb was hand-carried by a Confederate officer rather than mailed presumably because it contained $936, a small fortune in the war's waning days.

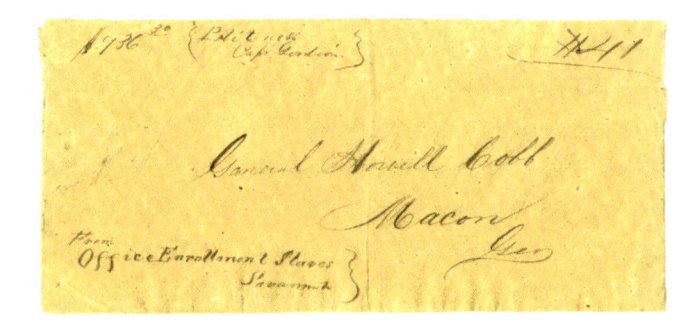

BLACK AMERICA FROM CIVIL WAR TO CIVIL RIGHTS

Mississippi sharecropper's cabin
COURTESY LIBRARY OF CONGRESS PRINTS AND PHOTOGRAPHS DIVISION

Reconstruction

1863–1877

Reconstruction refers to the process of reorganizing the southern states and readmitting them to the Union. It generally began once U.S. forces occupied a Confederate territory, and involved freeing local slaves and extending political rights to them. The rise of the Ku Klux Klan foreshadowed the difficulties that African Americans would face once the last federal forces withdrew from the south in 1877, leaving blacks vulnerable to segregationist "Jim Crow" laws.

▼ First Federal Issue revenue stamp on slave girl photograph c. 1864

The National Freedmen's Relief Association sold a series of slave photographs to raise money for educational projects in occupied New Orleans. They favored images of obviously mixed-race children, which appealed to a white audience. Photographs were taxed according to their retail value, and a government revenue stamp is found on the reverse.

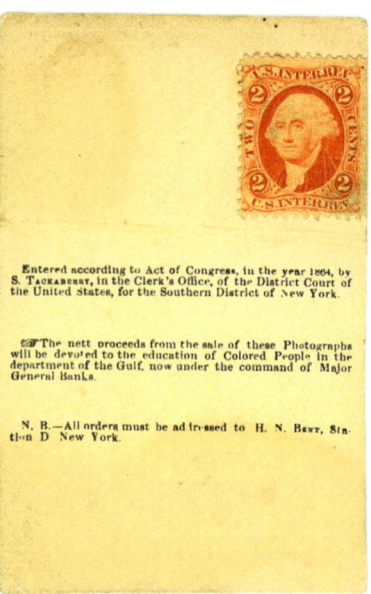

▶ Baltimore Association cover c. 1865

Addressee Rebecca Primus was an African American teacher from Connecticut brought south by the "Baltimore Association for the Moral and Education Improvement of the Colored People" to open a school for freed blacks in eastern Maryland.

Freedom Just Around the Corner

▾ Freedmen's Bureau cover c. 1865–1872

Private charity could only partially meet former slaves' needs, which ranged from food and clothing to employment and education. Congress created the Freedmen's Bureau in 1865 with Major General Oliver O. Howard as its commissioner. A Medal of Honor recipient, he later served as president of Howard University. His signature indicated that no postage was due.

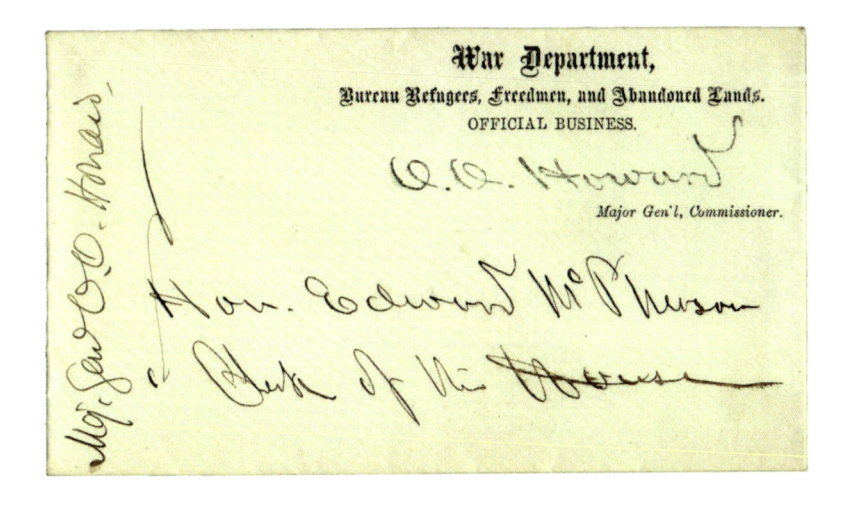

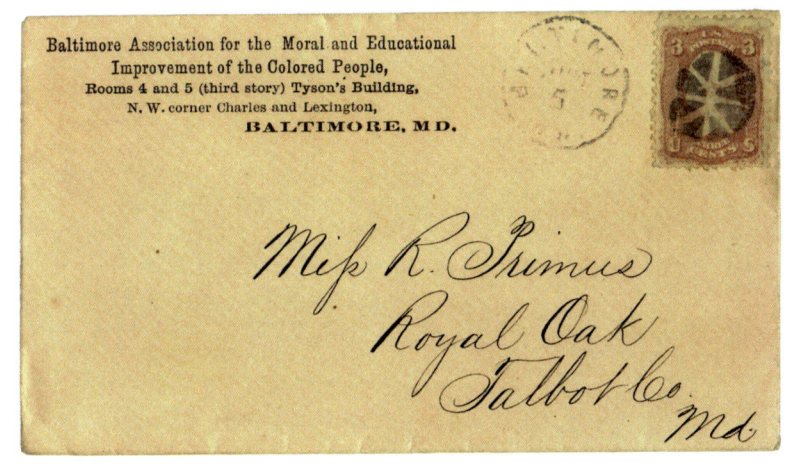

BLACK AMERICA FROM CIVIL WAR TO CIVIL RIGHTS

CONTRACT FOR LABOR.

State of Alabama,
COUNTY OF _Bullock_

Between _James W. Crews_, and the undersigned colored laborers, WITNESSETH, That I _James W. Crews_, obligate myself to give to the undersigned colored laborers, _One fourth the (¼)_ of the cotton; (⅛) of the corn; (⅛) of the fodder; and _¼ (¼)_ of all other produce raised on my plantation; and to furnish the said laborers with _Everything necessary to make a crop, say Land Stock Feed &c_ and _(3)¼_ pounds of good pork or bacon; and _One Peck_ of corn meal, each, per week, until the first day of January, 1869. _for full hand_

For and in consideration of the above, We, the undersigned colored laborers, obligate ourselves to labor faithfully for _James W. Crews_ _and half of every Saturday_ each day, from sunrise until sunset Sunday, excepted, until the first day of January, 1869, working according to, and obeying all reasonable orders given by the employer or his agent. We also obligate ourselves to pay _50 cts_ per day, for all time lost by us, _in case of breakup or other causes but at least willfully or without_ and to observe and be governed by the general rules and regulations of the plantation.

Signed at _Montgomery_ Ala., the _1st_ day of _March_, 1868.
Each head of family or single hand shall have one extra piece of land

J W Crews

Stephen X Crews   Frank X Mathews
Ben X Crews   Henry X Siler
Lewis X Crews   Peter X Mathews
Sallie X Crews   Wm X Mathews
Harriet X Crews   Hack X Mathews
John X Davis   Victoria X Siler
Sandy X Crews   Betsey X Siler
WITNESS: Albert X Crews   Emely X Siler
        Braughman X Fitzpatrick
        Sam X Crews
        Marshall X Mathews
        Henry X Mathews

◀ First Federal Issue revenue stamps on sharecropping contract MARCH 6, 1868 LOAN FROM MICHAEL MAHLER

Southern landowners no longer owned slaves, and most freedmen owned no land. This dilemma resulted in the sharecropping system, in which free blacks (and many poor whites) farmed someone else's land in return for one-quarter to two-thirds of the crop, depending on how much the landowner was obligated to provide for them.

▲ Buffalo Soldiers cover
OCTOBER 5, 1884 LOAN FROM CALVIN N. MITCHELL

A number of African American veterans chose to remain in the army after the Civil War. They were organized into four segregated regiments known collectively as the "Buffalo Soldiers." Colonel Benjamin Grierson, the white commander of the 10th U.S. Cavalry Regiment, sent this letter to his wife from the regiment's headquarters at Fort Davis, Texas.

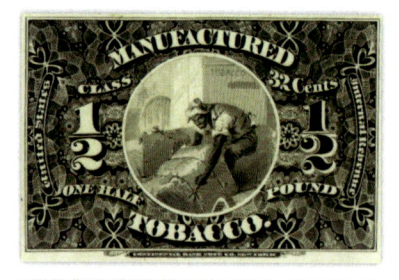

Long before famous African Americans were celebrated on postage stamps, poor black sharecroppers appeared on a series of revenue stamps issued to collect the tax on one of their major crops—tobacco. Similar images appeared on banknotes and checks of the period.

◂ **1/2 lb., 3 lb., and 5 lb. tobacco taxpaid stamps** 1868

▾ **1/2 lb. tobacco taxpaid revenue die essay** 1868

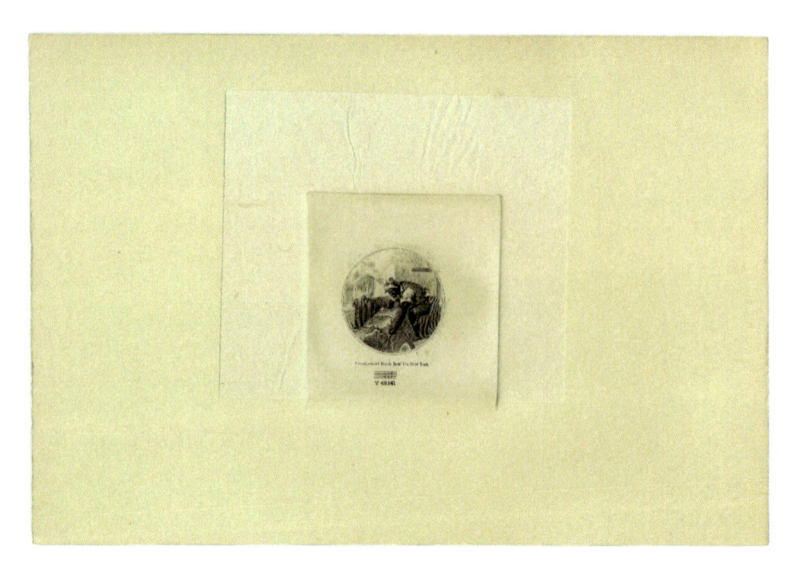

Freedom Just Around the Corner

Ku Klux Klan hood and mask c. 1990
LOAN FROM THE SOUTHERN POVERTY LAW CENTER COLLECTION OF REGALIA DONATED BY FORMER KLAN MEMBERS

Former slaves hoping to enjoy new-found freedom were soon confronted by whites trying to maintain their supremacy. The KKK began as a society of Confederate veterans that used terrorism to intimidate freedmen. Its most recognizable symbol—the pointed hood and mask—did not become common until the 1920s, however.

Most U.S. postmasters were not issued standard devices for canceling stamps until the 1890s. Prior to that, they were purchased from vendors or homemade. A number of hand-carved KKK-themed cancels were used by the post office at Union Mills, Pennsylvania in 1870. They serve as a reminder that the Klan had adherents in the north as well as the south.

▲ **"Skull and Crossbones" KKK postal cancel, Union Mills, Pennsylvania** c. 1870

LOAN FROM STAMPVESTORS LLC COMPLIMENTS OF COLUMBIAN STAMP COMPANY

The skull and crossbones was one of the earliest symbols adopted by the Klan.

▸ **Watertown, New York Ku Klux Klan**
c. 1870

COURTESY LIBRARY OF CONGRESS PRINTS AND PHOTOGRAPHS DIVISION

52   *Freedom Just Around the Corner*

▲ **"Kleagle Mask" KKK postal cancel, Union Mills, Pennsylvania** c. 1870
LOAN FROM STAMPVESTORS LLC COMPLIMENTS OF COLUMBIAN STAMP COMPANY

This cancel depicts an early style of homemade KKK mask. Modern stamp collectors refer to it as a *kleagle* mask after the title given to Klan recruiters, but that word was unknown in the 1870s.

◀ **Mississippi Ku-Klux, *Harper's Weekly***
JANUARY 27, 1872
COURTESY LIBRARY OF CONGRESS PRINTS AND PHOTOGRAPHS DIVISION

MISSISSIPPI KU-KLUX IN THE DISGUISES IN WHICH THEY WERE CAPTURED.
[FROM A PHOTOGRAPH.]

BLACK AMERICA FROM CIVIL WAR TO CIVIL RIGHTS   53

FIRST "JIM CROW" P.O. IN U.S

NORTH CAROLINA INSTITUTES SOMETHING NEW

(Associated Negro Press.)

Charlotte, N. C., July 17.—Something new under the sun has been found in North Carolina—a "Jim Crow" post office, where Negroes receive their mail from one pigeon hole, and the white people from another. One of Senator Simpson's constituents has sent to him a picture showing the dividing line between the white and Colored races at Makatoka, the Jim Crow office.

Makatoka is in Brunswick County, located in an isolated section, known as the Green Swamp Section, in the heart of a primeval forest of juniper and cypress.

"First 'Jim-Crow' P.O. in U.S.,"
Dallas *Express* JULY 19, 1919

Segregation

1877–1964

With the U.S. Army no longer suppressing the Klan and enforcing the political rights of freedmen, southern states introduced racial segregation and passed laws that made it difficult for black men to vote. Lynchings peaked between 1890 and 1910, and anti-lynching legislation became a perennial concern of new civil rights organizations such as the National Association for the Advancement of Colored People. Throughout this period, the post office and the military were the nation's largest employers, and they reflected the racial tensions of the larger society.

Postal Segregation

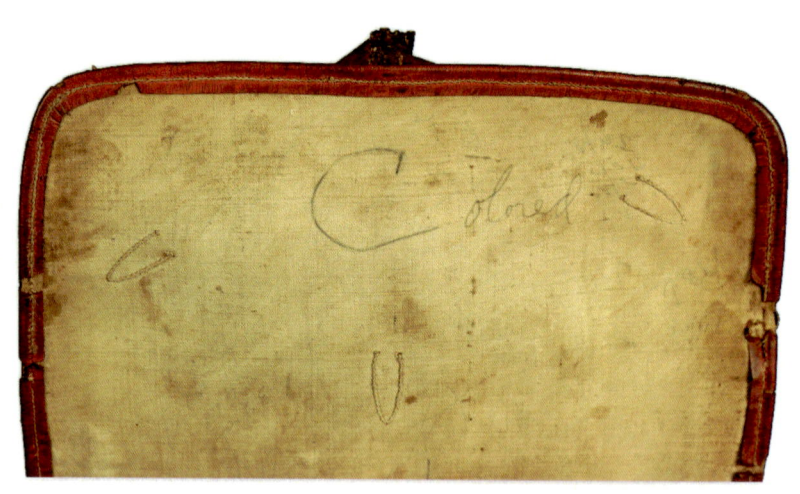

▸ **Segregated Rural Free Delivery saddlebag**
c. 1896

Palmyra, Virginia became a Rural Free Delivery post office on October 22, 1896, one of the first in the nation to deliver mail to farm families. This mailbag with separate compartments for "white" and "colored" mail was not required by federal policy but was procured by the carrier to satisfy either his own preferences or those of his customers.

▸ Account of the Frazer B. Baker lynching trial 1899
LOAN FROM AVERY RESEARCH CENTER, COLLEGE OF CHARLESTON

President William McKinley appointed hundreds of African American postmasters, including Frazer B. Baker of Lake City, South Carolina. Local whites burned the post office to force Baker to resign; when he did not, they burned his house and shot his family as they escaped. Because Baker was a U.S. government employee, his murder led to a federal trial. None of the accused was convicted, but the incident brought national attention to the lynching problem.

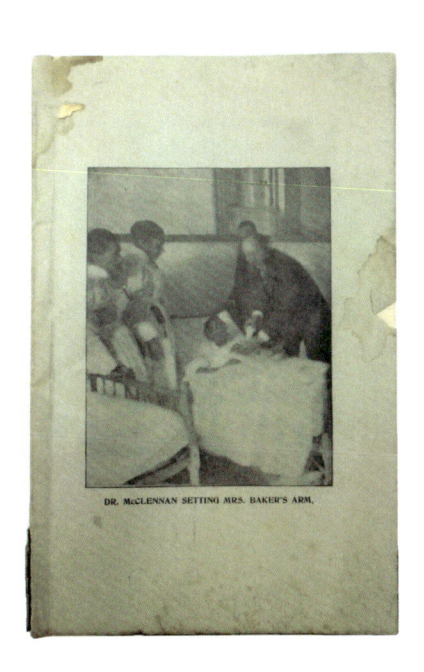

▾ Mrs. Frazer Baker and Children c. 1899
COURTESY LIBRARY OF CONGRESS PRINTS AND PHOTOGRAPHS DIVISION

▾ Blackdom, New Mexico post office cash book c. 1913

(FORM N.)

This Cash Book is for use at an Office Transacting Money Order Business on Domestic Basis Only.

CASH BOOK
OF THE
DOMESTIC MONEY ORDER OFFICE

At _Blackdom_ State of _N. Mex._
Beginning _April 1_ 191_3_
Ending _____ 191__

This book is the property of the United States. It is to be used EXCLUSIVELY as a Money Order Cash Book, and must be retained on file in the post office as a permanent record in the absence of instructions to the contrary.

Upon retiring from office the Postmaster must turn this Book over to his successor, together with all other Money Order records, blanks, and property, and transmit a receipt therefor to the Third Assistant Postmaster General (Division of Money Orders).

(TA Co. Edition April, 1913.)

Faced with segregation and discrimination in the east, many African Americans chose to establish their own towns in the west. Some, like Blackdom, grew large enough to support post offices that offered money orders and postal savings accounts, functioning as *de facto* banks. Cash books from these post offices contain the community's economic history.

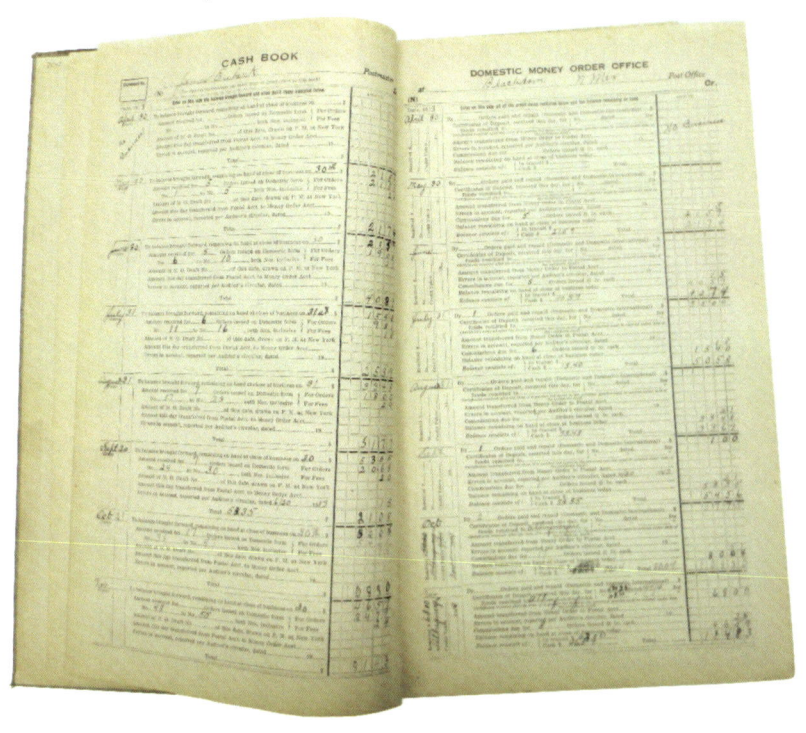

◀ Blackdom, New Mexico post office
c. 1913
COURTESY KNME-TV / CHANNEL 5

BLACK AMERICA FROM CIVIL WAR TO CIVIL RIGHTS 59

▼ The Postal Alliance NOVEMBER 1919
LOAN FROM MANUSCRIPT, ARCHIVES, AND RARE BOOK LIBRARY, EMORY UNIVERSITY

Federal employment was desegregated during Reconstruction. In 1913, however, President Woodrow Wilson resegregated the government. An early flash point was the Railway Mail Service (RMS), where close quarters and hazardous working conditions exacerbated racial tensions. Black RMS clerks formed the National Association of Postal Employees and published a journal, *The Postal Alliance,* to address their concerns.

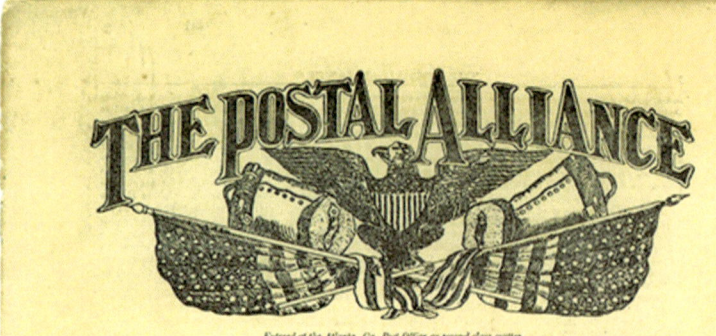

▲ **The Negro Motorist Green Book** 1966–1967 EDITION
LOAN FROM MANUSCRIPT, ARCHIVES, AND RARE BOOK LIBRARY, EMORY UNIVERSITY

Widespread discrimination and the prevalence of Jim Crow laws in the south made it difficult for African Americans to travel freely. Harlem, New York letter carrier Victor H. Green and his wife Alma published the *Green Book* from 1936 to 1966 to guide black travelers to hotels, restaurants, and other establishments that would serve them. Much of his information was supplied by fellow postal workers around the country.

Military Segregation

Let the black man get upon his person the brass letters U.S., let him get an eagle on his button, and a musket on his shoulder, and bullets in his pocket, and there is no power on earth or under the earth which can deny that he has earned the right of citizenship in the United States.

FREDERICK DOUGLASS, *SHOULD THE NEGRO ENLIST IN THE UNION ARMY?*, 1863

The idea of an entirely African American squadron in the Army Air Corps seemed far-fetched at a time when there were only a handful of black pilots in the entire country. However, Tuskegee Institute had operated a federally-funded training program for black pilots since 1939, so when just such a squadron was authorized by the War Department it was based there. Lieutenant Colonel Noel F. Parrish, the unit's third white commander, was directly responsible for ensuring the Tuskegee Airmen's many successes.

▾ Tuskegee aviation cadet Herbert O. Reid
cover APRIL 14, 1942

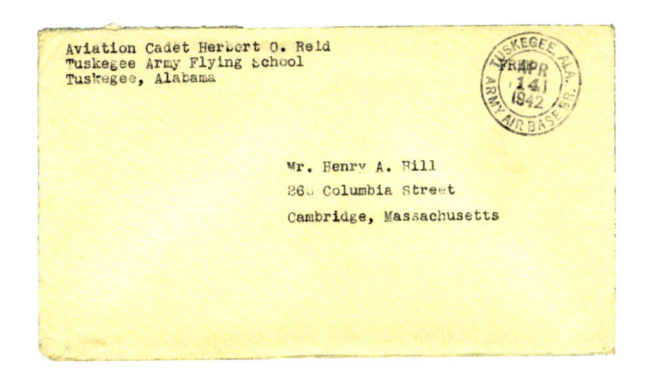

▾ Noel F. Parrish "somewhere in Alabama"
cover JULY 11, 1943

▾ 70¢ Charles Alfred Anderson approved stamp art by Sterling Hundley c. 2014

LOAN FROM THE UNITED STATES POSTAL SERVICE, POSTMASTER GENERAL'S COLLECTION

"Chief" Anderson was a self-taught Pennsylvania pilot who served as an instructor at the Tuskegee Army Air Field. His nickname stemmed from his title—Chief Civilian Flight Instructor. His students included two future African American four-star generals: Benjamin O. Davis, Jr. and Daniel "Chappie" James, Sr.

Freedom Just Around the Corner

▾ Marine 3rd Ammunition Company cover
JULY 13, 1945

One of the first all-black Marine units, the 3rd Ammunition Company's meritorious performance in the 1944 Battle of Saipan earned them a Presidential Unit Citation and won praise from senior white commanders, softening opposition to African Americans in the military.

▾ *The Crisis* magazine Editor-in-Chief cover
SEPTEMBER 28, 1944

African American soldiers in the field continued to receive, read, and correspond with black publications such as the NAACP's *The Crisis* magazine. The sender of this letter, Private First Class Sam Wallace, Jr. of Kansas, was killed in action in the final months of the war.

▾ Cover from "Walter White/War Correspondent"

MARCH 11, 1945

Longtime NAACP Executive Secretary Walter F. White served as a war correspondent for several publications, including the *New York Post*. He reported on the contributions of black military personnel and the discrimination they faced in the service. His book *A Rising Wind* figured in President Harry S. Truman's 1948 decision to desegregate the military.

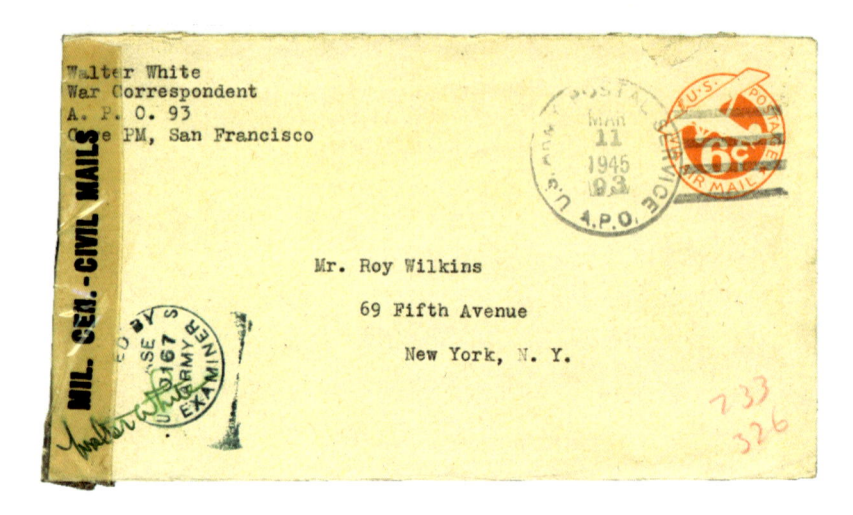

6888th Central Postal Battalion on parade in Rouen, France MAY 27, 1945
COURTESY NATIONAL ARCHIVES AND RECORDS ADMINISTRATION

The 6888th was the first all-black battalion in the Women's Army Corps, and the only such unit deployed overseas in World War II. Its 855 members were sent to England and France in 1945 to clear a backlog of undelivered mail addressed to U.S. soldiers serving in Europe.

Captain Dovey Johnson Roundtree jacket and insignia c. OCTOBER 1942–JUNE 1943

LOAN FROM NATIONAL PARK SERVICE, MARY MCLEOD BETHUNE COUNCIL HOUSE NATIONAL HISTORIC SITE

One of the first African American officers in the Women's Army Auxiliary Corps during World War II, Roundtree was known as a tireless recruiter. This uniform is an early style, worn before the WAACs converted to full military status and dropped "auxiliary" from their name on July 1, 1943.

V-Mail microfilm strip c. 1944

The U.S. military's V-Mail (short for Victory Mail) system involved photographing letters to military personnel, then sending the microfilmed negatives to be developed and delivered in the field. The top letter in this V-Mail microfilm strip is a letter from a Howard University student to her husband in the navy.

Street marchers in Harlem, New York MARCH 1965
COURTESY LIBRARY OF CONGRESS PRINTS AND PHOTOGRAPHS DIVISION

Few things can help an individual more than to place responsibility on him.

BOOKER T. WASHINGTON

Civil Rights Movement

The first generation of civil rights leaders were born in slavery or were the children of slaves. They emphasized education and self-reliance as the path to equality, founding local and national organizations to help fellow black Americans become educated, build businesses, and establish social networks. The institutions they created trained and nurtured later generations of activist leaders.

1867–1972

Education

▾ Mary McLeod Bethune to Walter White cover
OCTOBER 17, 1928

A notation on this envelope indicates that it contained a letter from Mary McLeod Bethune concerning the deadly 1928 Okeechobee Hurricane, in which 75% of those killed were poor black farmers in the lowlands surrounding Lake Okeechobee. Bethune founded Bethune-Cookman College at Daytona Beach, Florida in 1904.

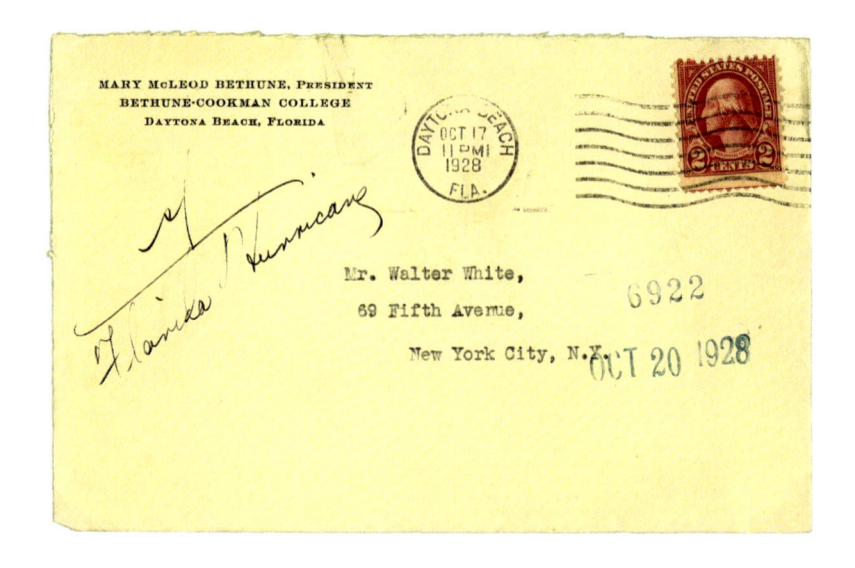

The Tuskegee Institute, which Booker T. Washington founded and where George Washington Carver taught for nearly a half-century, offered a practical education to future teachers, farmers, and industrial workers.

▼ Tuskegee Institute cover to Nigeria FEBRUARY 19, 1913

▼ 10¢ Booker T. Washington
1940

▶ 3¢ George Washington Carver block of four 1948

BLACK AMERICA FROM CIVIL WAR TO CIVIL RIGHTS   73

Publishing

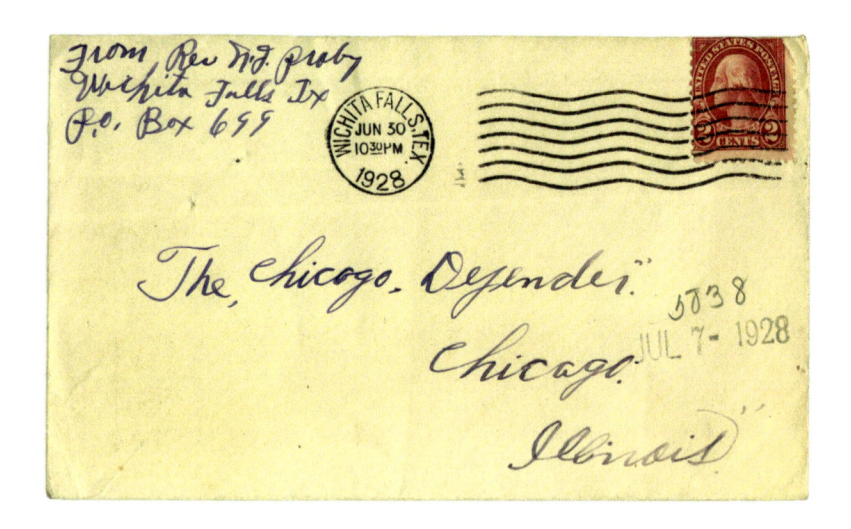

▲ ***The Chicago Defender* cover** JUNE 30, 1928

The Chicago Defender both encouraged and chronicled the "Great Migration" of African Americans to northern urban centers between 1910 and 1970. Despite its title, most of its readers were outside Chicago; black travelers frequently smuggled copies into the south, where many news agents refused to carry it.

Novelist, playwright, and poet Paul Laurence Dunbar was one of the first black writers to be accepted by the white literary establishment. He published pieces in *Atlantic Monthly*, *Harper's Weekly,* and *Saturday Evening Post* as well as writing *Dahomey,* the first African American Broadway musical.

▶ **10¢ Paul Laurence Dunbar imperforate pair** 1975
LOAN FROM JOHN M. HOTCHNER

▼ **Paul Laurence Dunbar cover** JUNE 11, 1895
LOAN FROM JOHN M. HOTCHNER

◀ ***The Call* black newspaper cover** FEBRUARY 17, 1944

In addition to national news items, Kansas City's *The Call* focused on printing social information that the city's white-owned newspapers declined to print, such as marriages, obituaries, and graduation announcements. NAACP Executive Director Roy Wilkins began his career as a reporter for *The Call.*

Organizations

▸ **National Negro Business League cover**
JULY 24, 1914

Organized in 1900 by Booker T. Washington, the National Negro Business League encouraged its members to cater to black consumers and advertise in black magazines and newspapers.

Charles Hamilton Houston founded the NAACP's legal department in 1935. For the next fifteen years he challenged segregation through the courts and mentored his successor, the future Supreme Court Justice Thurgood Marshall.

▸ **42¢ Charles Hamilton Houston and Walter White** 2009

▾ **Thurgood Marshall to Charles Hamilton Houston cover** SEPTEMBER 23, 1935

76   *Freedom Just Around the Corner*

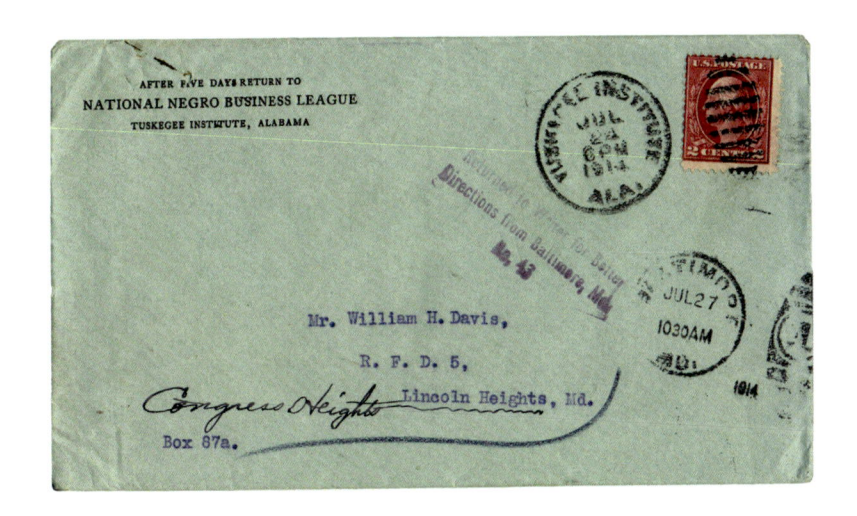

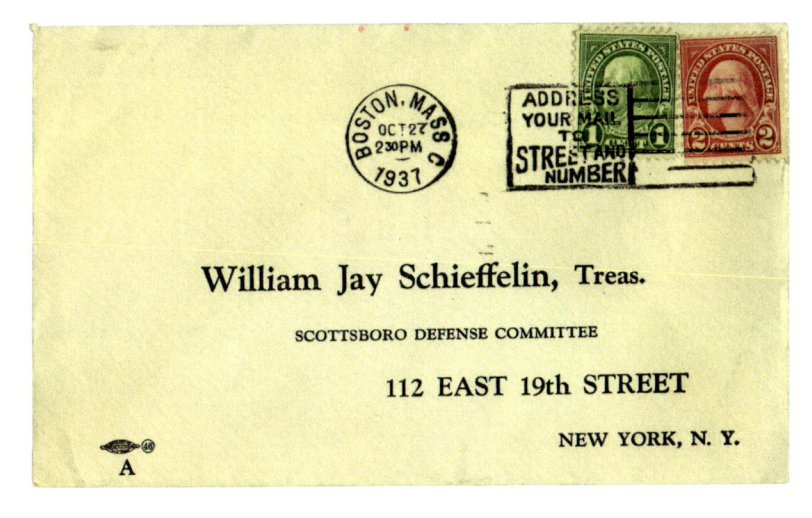

▲ Scottsboro Defense Committee cover
OCTOBER 27, 1937

The "Scottsboro Boys" were nine black teenagers from Alabama falsely convicted of raping two white teenage girls in 1931. The convictions were overturned by the Supreme Court and sent back to Alabama for retrial. The NAACP cooperated with the Scottsboro Defense Committee to raise money to pay for the Scottsboro Boys' defense, but five of them were reconvicted. All were eventually paroled or pardoned.

The Struggle Against Lynching

78 *Freedom Just Around the Corner*

◀ **Ida B. Wells approved stamp art by Thomas Blackshear II**
C. 1990 LOAN FROM THE UNITED STATES POSTAL SERVICE, POSTMASTER GENERAL'S COLLECTION

Born a slave in Mississippi during the Civil War, Ida B. Wells became a journalist and lecturer who brought worldwide attention to race issues in the United States. She undertook the first systematic, statistical study that exposed the lynching problem.

Ruby Hurley opened the NAACP's first permanent office in Alabama in 1951. She investigated the murders of several African Americans, including fifteen-year-old Emmet Till, before turning her attention to the desegregation of public universities.

▶ **42¢ Ella Baker and Ruby Hurley**
2009

▼ **Home Missions Council to Ruby Hurley cover** SEPTEMBER 18, 1951

BLACK AMERICA FROM CIVIL WAR TO CIVIL RIGHTS

The Rise of Direct Action

During the 1950s, legal and political challenges to segregation were replaced by non-violent "direct action" tactics such as boycotts, sit-ins, and marches. This was due in part to the influence of World War II veterans, who had fought for freedom abroad and were no longer willing to accept less at home. The largest and most famous of these demonstrations was the August 1963 March on Washington for Jobs and Freedom, the setting for Martin Luther King's *I Have a Dream* speech.

▸ **"Full Freedom by 1963" cover** JANUARY 7, 1957

The slogan on this NAACP envelope refers to the organization's stated goal of equality for African Americans by the 100th anniversary of the Emancipation Proclamation. The centennial was also the occasion of the March on Washington.

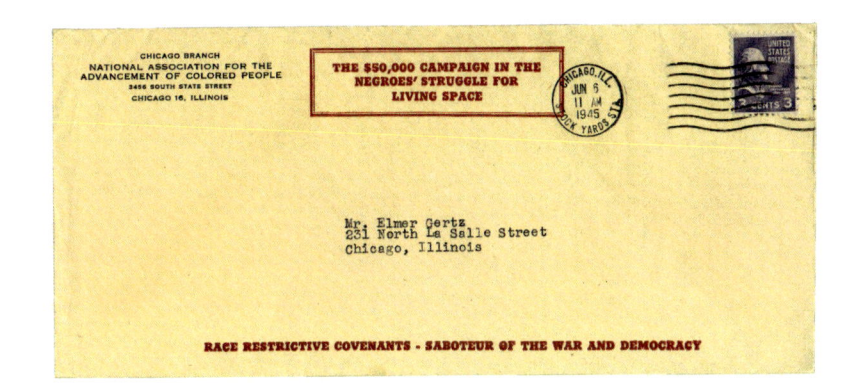

▲ Chicago NAACP Race Restrictive Covenants cover
JUNE 6, 1945

As America suburbanized from the 1920s to the 1960s, black Americans were excluded from buying homes in many communities. The NAACP addressed this trend at the end of World War II, when returning black veterans were entitled to low cost G.I. Bill mortgages but found it difficult to buy property.

▾ White House cover to A. Philip Randolph
DECEMBER 3, 1962

Labor leader A. Philip Randolph first proposed a mass protest in Washington, D.C. during 1941. Although it never materialized, he participated in planning for the August 1963 March on Washington. This envelope dates from a period when the Kennedy administration was discouraging the march's organizers from going through with it.

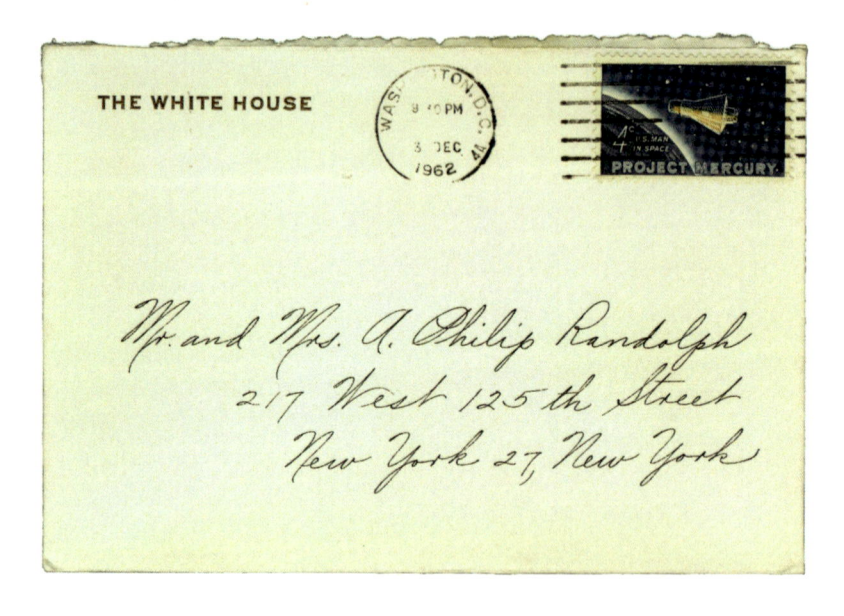

▲ **33¢ Martin Luther King, Jr. approved stamp art by Keith Birdsong** c. 1999

LOAN FROM THE UNITED STATES POSTAL SERVICE, POSTMASTER GENERAL'S COLLECTION

Martin Luther King's *I Have a Dream* speech was commemorated in the Postal Service's Celebrate the Century stamp series issued at the end of the twentieth century. A trace of brightness on the horizon represents hope, while King wears the March's official badge.

BLACK AMERICA FROM CIVIL WAR TO CIVIL RIGHTS

▼ "Mrs. Medgar Evers" cover
JUNE 14, 1963

The March on Washington occurred between two infamous civil rights crimes. NAACP leader Medgar Evers was assassinated in Jackson, Mississippi two months before the March; less than a month afterward, four young girls died in a bombing at Birmingham, Alabama's 16th Street Baptist Church. This cover contained a letter of condolence to Myrlie Evers-Williams, who later became chairman of the NAACP.

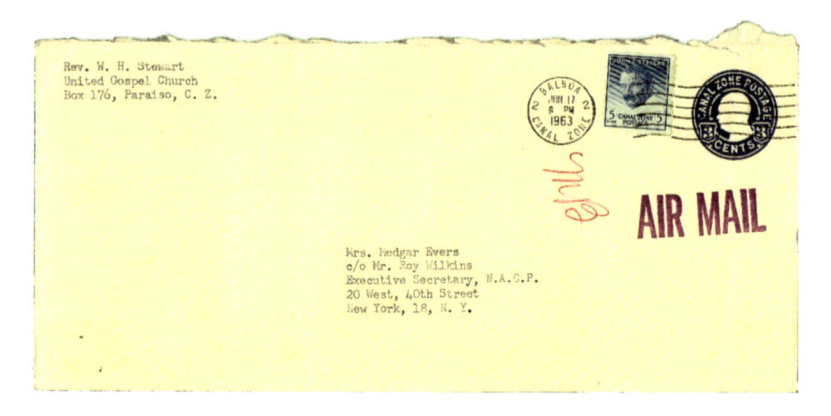

▶ 42¢ Medgar Evers and Fannie Lou Hamer 2009

84 *Freedom Just Around the Corner*

Political Pins c. 1960s–1970s
LOAN FROM TUSKEGEE UNIVERSITY ARCHIVES

The images and slogans on these lapel pins symbolize the "Black Power" movement that gained popularity in the years after the March on Washington. It went beyond the equality called for by the mainstream civil rights movement, instead emphasizing a sense of racial pride.

First day covers of the Booker T. Washington commemorative stamp being cancelled at Tuskegee Institute, Alabama APRIL 7, 1940

COURTESY SMITHSONIAN INSTITUTION LIBRARIES

The Black Heritage stamps reflect the progress, richness, and diversity of African American achievements.

U.S. POSTAL SERVICE

Black Heritage Stamp Series

U.S. postage stamps were in use for nearly a century before Booker T. Washington became the first African American to appear on one. A handful of additional black history-related designs appeared between 1940 and 1978, when the U.S. Postal Service introduced the Black Heritage series. Today the Black Heritage issues are the longest-running U.S. stamp series.

1978-Present

▸ 25¢ Frederick Douglass approved stamp art by Walter DuBois Richards
c. 1967

The Douglass stamp marked the first time an African American was included in a "regular" stamp series; that is, one meant for everyday postal use. The dramatic portrait was based on a photograph approved by Douglass's descendants.

▾ 5¢ Emancipation Proclamation concept stamp art by Georg Olden c. 1963

This bold, allegorical commemorative for the hundredth anniversary of the Emancipation Proclamation was the first U.S. postage stamp designed by an African American.

Freedom Just Around the Corner

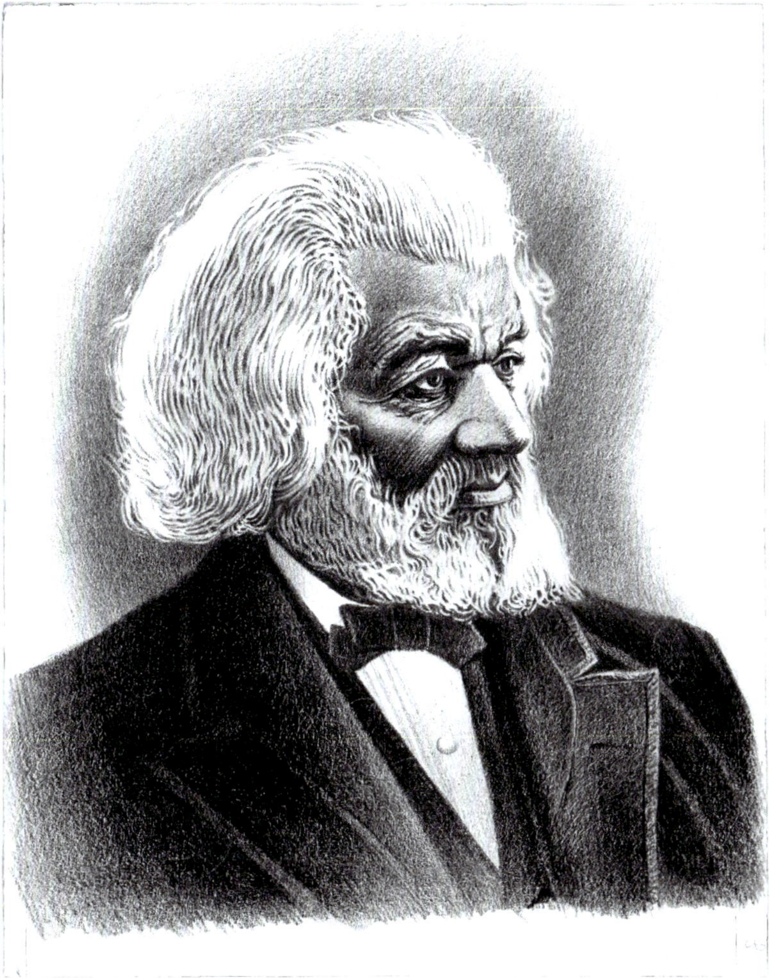

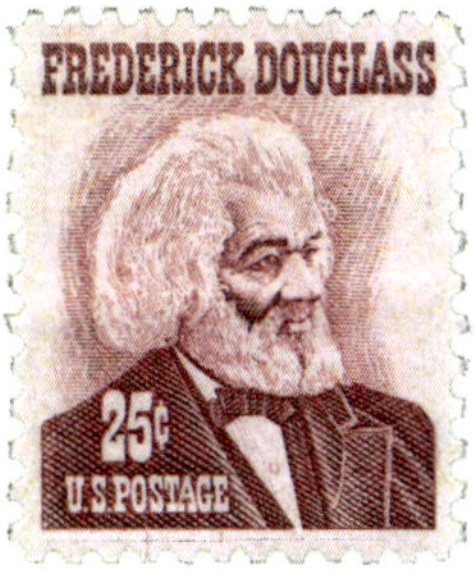
FREDERICK DOUGLASS
25¢
U.S.POSTAGE

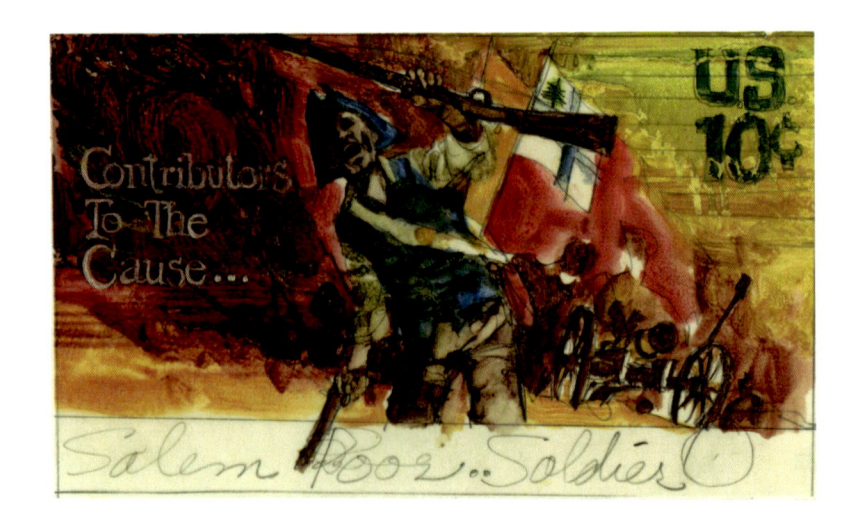

▲ 10¢ Salem Poor concept stamp art by Neil Boyle
c. 1975

The U.S. bicentennial was the occasion for this stamp, part of a series that honored little-known figures of the American Revolution. Salem Poor was a slave who purchased his freedom and later participated in the battles at Bunker Hill, Valley Forge, and White Plains.

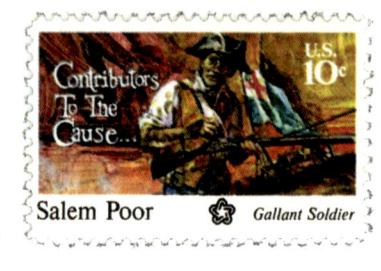

◄ *Spirit of '76* Political Pin
c. 1974

LOAN FROM TUSKEGEE UNIVERSITY ARCHIVES

90   *Freedom Just Around the Corner*

DEPARTMENT OF THE TREASURY
BUREAU OF ENGRAVING AND PRINTING

For Approval of Engraving and Provisional
Approval of the Color:
Final color approval to be given on Press Sheet

Illustrator Jerry Pinkney's designs for the first Black Heritage stamps set the tone for the series and were emulated by later illustrators Thomas Blackshear II and Higgins Bond. They feature a central portrait surrounded by symbolic vignettes of the subject's primary accomplishments.

▲ **13¢ Harriet Tubman die proof** c. 1978

▸ **15¢ Martin Luther King, Jr. approved stamp art by Jerry Pinkney** c. 1979

BLACK AMERICA FROM CIVIL WAR TO CIVIL RIGHTS

Controversies

The Black Heritage series has occasionally drawn criticism, especially when it has depicted individuals who espoused controversial political ideologies.

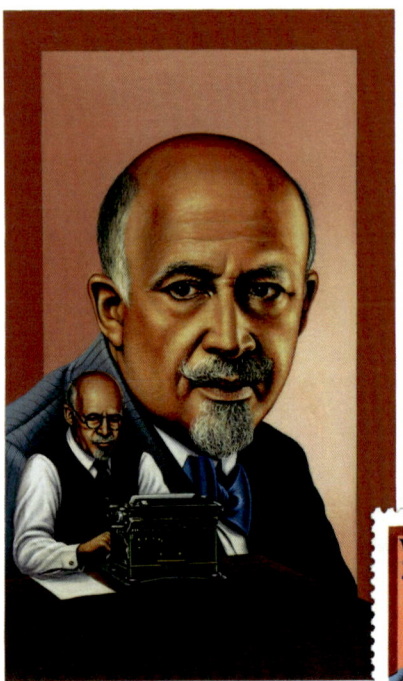

◄ 29¢ W. E. B. Du Bois approved stamp art by Higgins Bond c. 1992

Targeted during the McCarthy era for his socialist views, W. E. B. Du Bois accepted Ghanaian citizenship and formally joined the Communist Party at the age of 93. Some critics felt that this should have prevented his appearance on a U.S. stamp.

▶ 33¢ Malcolm X concept stamp art by Chris Calle c. 1999

Criticism of the 1999 Black Heritage stamp honoring Malcom X centered on his early association with the Nation of Islam and his controversial view that blacks should advance civil rights "by any means necessary," including violence.

BLACK AMERICA FROM CIVIL WAR TO CIVIL RIGHTS

Portraiture

The Black Heritage series has always commemorated people rather than organizations or events. As a result, its attraction lies in the strength of its portraiture. This presents challenges when representing early subjects for whom there are few source images, but it has also produced stunning and memorable artwork.

◄ 22¢ Jean Baptiste Point du Sable approved stamp art by Thomas Blackshear II c. 1987

There are no extant portraits of Chicago pioneer du Sable or his cabin; other artists' conceptions inspired Blackshear's haunting portrait.

▸ 37¢ Marian Anderson approved stamp art by Albert Slark c. 2005

Canadian-born artist Albert Slark created this full-color oil portrait of Marian Anderson from a circa 1934 black-and-white photograph. Easily one of the most beautiful designs in the Black Heritage series, it won numerous awards and was exhibited at the Society of Illustrators 48th Annual Exhibition in New York City.

94   *Freedom Just Around the Corner*

BLACK AMERICA FROM CIVIL WAR TO CIVIL RIGHTS

Legacies

Due in part to the success of the Black Heritage series, since the 1980s there has been a substantial increase in the number of African American subjects included in other series.

Legends of American Music Series

▲ **29¢ Nat "King" Cole approved stamp art by C. F. Payne** c. 1994

Known for his melodic baritone voice, Cole was the first African American entertainer to have his own television variety show.

Performing Arts Series

◄ **22¢ Duke Ellington approved stamp art by Jim Sharpe** c. 1986

The most prolific jazz composer ever, Edward "Duke" Ellington and his orchestra toured the U.S. for nearly fifty years and also popularized the genre in Europe.

BLACK AMERICA FROM CIVIL WAR TO CIVIL RIGHTS

Literary Arts Series

▲ **37¢ Zora Neale Hurston approved stamp art by Drew Struzan** c. 2003

A noted folklorist, novelist and anthropologist, Hurston is best known for her 1937 novel, *Their Eyes Were Watching God*.

Distinguished Americans Series

▸ **23¢ Wilma Rudolph approved stamp art by Mark Summers** c. 2004

Rudolph won three gold medals in track at the 1960 Olympic Games in Rome, despite having contracted infantile paralysis (polio) at the age of four.

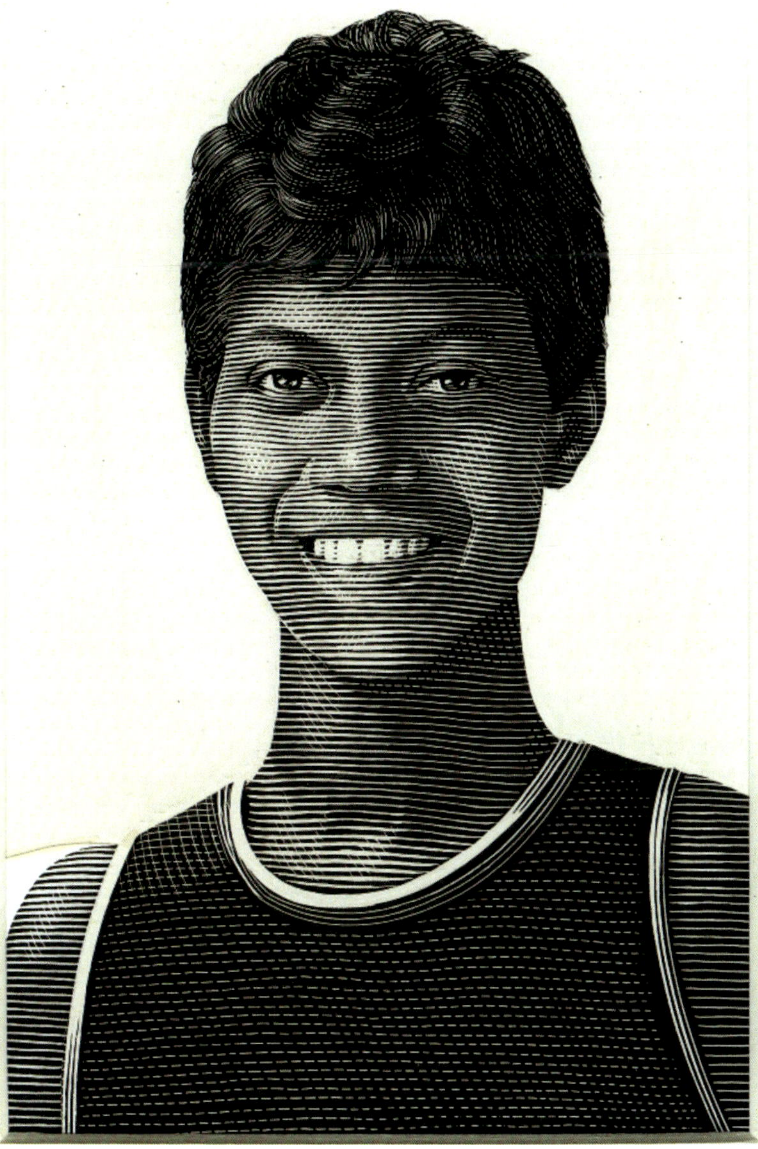

Curator's Afterword

Freedom Just Around the Corner is intended to commemorate the 150th anniversaries of the end of the Civil War and total abolition in the United States, as well as to celebrate the impending addition of the National Museum of African American History and Culture to the Smithsonian family. I think we have created a worthy tribute to these occasions.

In selecting the fifty or so NPM pieces that form the backbone of this exhibition, I was impressed by our collection's strength in covers mailed to and by great figures in black history. It quickly became apparent that these were transferred to us by the Manuscript Division of the Library of Congress in the 1970s and 1980s. Today's exhibitions are always indebted to the foresight of previous generations of curators and administrators.

While I am on the subject of indebtedness, a curator accumulates many debts in the course of staging an exhibit such as *Freedom*. Without a doubt, my two largest creditors are Marvin Murray and Assistant Curator of Philately Calvin Mitchell. Marvin's first-hand knowledge of twentieth-century military history helped to identify several important covers shown in the Military Segregation section of the exhibit, and he arranged our interviews with General and Mrs. Brown and Col. McQuillan for the audio portion of the exhibit.

Calvin indefatigably tracked down artifacts that I wanted on loan and commented thoughtfully on more versions of the exhibit script than he probably cares to remember. He cheerfully embraced the audio interview component of the project, even though it evolved late in the game. He worked on this project as a volunteer for more than a year before we were able to bring him on staff, and I am deeply grateful to him for his advice and dedication.

What a pleasure it was to be able to draw on the Postmaster General's Collection of original U.S. stamp art, on permanent loan to the National Postal Museum since 2010! Having this collection on hand allowed us to trace the history of the Black Heritage series. In addition, Cindy Tackett and Bill Gicker of USPS graciously worked to get us the 2014 C. Alfred "Chief" Anderson artwork ahead of schedule so it could be featured in this show.

DANIEL A. PIAZZA
CHIEF CURATOR OF PHILATELY

Message from ESPER

The Ebony Society of Philatelic Events and Reflections (ESPER) is an international community of stamp collectors who encourage and support Black people in all their philatelic pursuits, especially the study of stamps and philatelic material related to the African Diaspora.

ESPER was pleased to provide support for this first-ever Smithsonian exhibition devoted entirely to African American philately and history. Many of our members contributed items and expertise to this project, including Karen Bertha, John Hotchner, David Mielke, and Calvin Mitchell.

We hope this exhibition will inspire you to start or revive your own collection of stamps. If so, please consider joining the nearly 300 ESPER members throughout the United States and in other countries who read our award-winning quarterly newsletter, *Reflections*, and gather at shows for fellowship and philately.

Visit our website at esperstamps.org or write to ESPER, Box 1757, Lincolnton Station, New York NY 10037-1757.

WALTER LEE FAISON, JR.
PRESIDENT

Acknowledgements

Freedom Just Around the Corner was staged through the combined efforts of a very talented exhibit team that included Eric Chapman, Exhibits; Marshall Emery, Public Relations; Motoko Hioki, Education; Manda Kowalczyk, Conservation; Patricia Raynor, Collections; Elizabeth Schorr, Collections; Roxanne Symko Smith, Project Manager; and Allie Swislocki, Advancement. Many NPM staff worked on various aspects of the project, including Polone Bazile, Finance; Amy Borntrager, Advancement; Linda Edquist, Conservation; Lynn Heidelbaugh, Curatorial; Rebecca Kennedy, Conservation; Sharon Klotz, Exhibits; Bill Lommel, Web Design; Hannah Molofsky, Special Events; James O'Donnell, Collections; Kim Skerritt, Education; and Kim Wayman, Contracting.

We are especially grateful to our donor-sponsors, including Guido Craveri; The Perry Hansen Family; Pitney Bowes; and the Ebony Society of Philatelic Events and Reflections. Publication of this exhibition catalogue was supported by the George W. Brett Philatelic Publications Endowment Fund.

This exhibition was greatly enriched by numerous pieces generously loaned from institutions and private collectors, including Avery Research Center, College of Charleston; Carl J. Cruz; Manuscript, Archives, and Rare Book Library, Emory University; John M. Hotchner; Howard County (MD) Historical Society; Hermann Ivester; Patrick Maselis; David Mielke; Calvin N. Mitchell; National Park Service, Mary McLeod Bethune Council House National Historic Site; Smithsonian Institution Libraries, Dibner Library of the History of Science and Technology; Smithsonian Institution Libraries, National Postal Museum Library; Southern Poverty Law Center; Stampvestors LLC through Columbian Stamp Company; Scott R. Trepel; Tuskegee University

Archives; and United States Postal Service, Postmaster General's Collection.

Several individuals kindly consented to be interviewed for the audio component of the exhibit, adding a personal dimension to object interpretation. Interviewees were Dr. Fostenia Baker; Karen Bertha; Dr. Francoise B. Bonnell, Director, U.S. Army Women's Museum; Lt. Gen. Earl Brown (USAF Ret.); Gloria Brown; Dr. Rhea Combs, Curator of Photography and Film, Smithsonian National Museum of African American History and Culture; Carl J. Cruz; Linda Edquist, Conservator, Smithsonian National Postal Museum; Lynn Heidelbaugh, Curator, Smithsonian National Postal Museum; Tina Jones; Col. James McQuillan (USAF Ret.); Michael Newton; and Scott R. Trepel.

Others who contributed to the exhibit's success were Christine Lefebvre, *Freedom's* designer; Smithsonian Institution Office of Exhibits Central, graphics printing; and Jayne Girod Holt and Catherine Valentour, contract conservators. Minuteman Press of Toledo, Ohio printed the exhibition catalogue.

Images, audio, and video came from many sources, including Carl J. Cruz; Library of Congress Prints and Photographs Division; Library of Congress Recorded Sound Reference Center; National Archives and Records Administration; NBCUniversal; and Smithsonian Institution Libraries, National Postal Museum Library.

We must strive for the rights which the world accords to men.

W.E.B. DU BOIS